POEMS

Sun and Rain/The Flowery Country/Grains of Sand

Tan Kheng Yeang

Order this book online at www.trafford.com
or email orders@trafford.com

Most Trafford titles are also available at major online book retailers.

Printed in the United States of America.

ISBN: 978-1-4269-9268-1 (sc)
ISBN: 978-1-4269-9269-8 (hc)
ISBN: 978-1-4269-9270-4 (e)

Library of Congress Control Number: 2011963566

Trafford rev. 07/13/2012

 www.trafford.com

North America & international
toll-free: 1 888 232 4444 (USA & Canada)
phone: 250 383 6864 ♦ fax: 812 355 4082

Other books by the same author

Fiction

Novels
Conflict in the Home
Sauce of Life
Struggle Toward Extinction
Motivating Forces

Poetry
Diverse Modes

Non-Fiction

Memoir
Dark Days

Philosophy
Intrinsic to Universe
The Material Structure

Sayings
Reduced Reflections

Linguistics
LUIF: A New Language

Acknowledgement

"The author wishes to thank Ms. Valerie Cameron for her invaluable assistance in preparing the manuscript of this book for publication."

Contents

By the author of *Diverse Modes* and *Reduced Reflections*, this volume consists of three anthologies spanning a range of poetic styles.

Sun and Rain follows the style and philosophy of the great Romantic poets, extolling the wonders and terrors of nature and the exploring the depths of human emotion. The author paints vivid and moving pictures that are swept along by the lyrical meter and rhyme of traditional verse.

The Flowery Country is an exploration of the currents of history that shaped the venerable Chinese culture. However, unlike traditional history, which is dry and dispassionate, this work resonates with emotion, ideas, and imagination. Written in a new literary style developed by the author called "amorphous verse," which does not differ from prose in style but retains the lyricism of poetry in terms of language, *The Flowery Country* propels readers through the colourful sweep of emperors, dynasties, love, and war, leaving them to ponder the vicissitude of human nature.

Grains of Sand is a study of human nature and the creations of humankind expressed in verse. The horrors of war, the tenderness of love, and the joy of cherished memories are juxtaposed with small, keenly observed gems of everyday life and objects, which, like a photograph, are forever caught in time by the pen of the poet.

SUN AND RAIN

In the Rain

Reeling in wildest dance,
   The fresh rain flashes down,
     Fleet in its subtle sweep;
I have been caught by chance
   Along this road, which sleep
Has wreathed in a ripe trance
   Erewhile, but now is grown
     A place where runnels creep.

What songs its bright drops weave,
   So exquisitely sweet;
     The numerous tunes and tones
In swift succession cleave
   The air with passionate moans;
From forth all corners heave
   Canorous sounds, which greet
     My ear like lulling drones.

It bathes me as I go,
   Till I am blithely cold—
     Luxurious joy I feel,
Which makes my bosom glow!
   Great waves of happiness steal
Through all my being now;
   What blossomy thrills enfold
     My mind, which seems to reel!

My feverish heart allays
   Its passions with their stings:
     A balmy rapture fills,
My frame with genial rays,
   And bliss so richly trills
On me that all the days
   Of care are flown, and flings
     My mind off all its ills.

From my long pent-up pain
   I feel a full relief
      I scarcely can define:
In all my heart and brain
   A rippling joy is mine,
Hearing the rolling rain,
   Which flows with eloquent grief
      In a perennial line.

Afresh all things begin
   Beneath the magical brush
      Of the cloud-fallen rain,
Which makes the landscape win
   An odorous life again;
All objects seem to spin
   With rapture, as they flush
      With water they retain.

Shrilly I hear it sound
   The secret of its life:
      How, wandering through the air,
Burrowing into the ground,
   Or steaming to its lair
Near heaven, peace around
   It never smiles, but strife
      Must it forever bear.

Type of the deep unrest,
   Which permeates Nature's soul,
      I throb in sympathy
With it—I, in whose breast
   Is like a victory
Of tumult—fiery pest;
   Beneath its rhythmic roll
      Praise of it girdles me.

A Peal of Thunder

The flashing gold of lightning floats and thrills
    Through the tempestuous air thick showers fall,
    Weaving grand subtle songs swift winds enthral
The earth, which their unceasing music fills,
Dark clouds on high enwrap the distant hills,
    The sky appears a desolate, grey wall,
    The garrulous cries of rocking thunder call
The place to passionate life—it fumes and shrills;
The air is trembling with a sudden peal
    Of thunder, which the clouds appear to fling
    Out of their caves, and which shoots a sharp ring
So strongly that it makes my spirit reel
With wild, ineffable joy! I seem to feel
    The scene around unveil its heart and sing!

To a Storm

Though you sing of the rocking gloom of the trees,
    Which wave their leaves in tune to your song;
    And the flaunting sun, which all day long
Has shone, now swooning in swift degrees;
And dizzy desponding of the seas
    Of clouds which float—a desolate throng;

And of grief, which, flowing from your core
    And diffused along your wandering wings,
    Engirdles the scenery and flings
Its feverish tones at the foaming floor
Of the sky, like one who never more
    Will taste joy from Hope's celestial springs;

Yet to me more dulcetly you sound
    Than the tremulous murmuring of the rills,
    Or the music, which the sea distils
From its radiant waves, as they flow and bound,
Or the tinkling runnels, which surround
    The inspiring morning from blissful bills;

For can your bitter notes not be sweet
    To me, whose mind is as sad as your own?
    A chaotic eddy of tumult, sown
With torturing thoughts! Despair's stern seat!
But now it glows with ethereal heat,
    As into me your spirit has flown.

Within me the deep distress that burns
    Is vigorous and intensely keen;
    Caustic weariness comes between
My spirit and rapturous peace, for which yearns
My heart; and it always—alas!—returns
    As freshly as if it had not been;

For my soul is deeply weary of things
    And loves to browse on measureless gloom,
    Bearing within it a crushing doom
Of misery—that is why it clings
To your groaning song, which happily flings
    Some harmony into its clamorous room.

Though grief is hard to endure and its glow,
    Not ephemeral—hard to be effaced—
    Yet a spirit, stern as yours, may be braced
To embower it easily, and not allow
Itself to be quenched by this weight of woe,
    This frightful fardel it has encased.

Then blow still more furious, wafting here
    All the shrill melodies, which arise
    From your flexuous motion; how fleetly flies
Your liquid stream! Oh that you would rear
A song severer still, and could wear
    A visible presence, austere as your sighs.

Oh august proclaimer of Nature's grief!
    Chanting there in your furious pain
    And dragging despair and gloom in your train!
Oh example of Nature's passion! Chief
Of the sad! You who bring my troubles relief!
    How my spirit is kindled by your strain!

As you roll along in your sinuous course,
    Your wings apparel the earth and breed
    Sympathy in the scene; as you speed,
Heaven is sombre and deplores
That the clouds are darkened to their cores:
    But oh! How my soul you can fill and feed!

The Crowd

What a numerous throng has assembled here
    To jostle—vociferate—laugh!
    The illumined field is rough
With a crowd so colossal it is clear
    Some attraction gigantic enough
Must have lured them to drop together so near!

The place is ringing with voices that flow
    Around, a bewildering din;
    What glorious wonder can win
Over this wavering multitude, so
    Dizzy with rapture, in
Such ebullient joy? A public show!

All the days of this multitude jostle and flame
    With perennial, staggering strife,
    Which rattles and thunders through life,
As they ceaselessly hunt their ignoble aim—
    To render their time more rife
With what futile pleasures they can claim.

Their ardent wishes do not concern
    The lofty, exquisite things
    To which simplicity brings
Such rapture as they can never learn.
    What fatiguing fever clings
To their souls and makes their bosoms burn.

All day they fidget with sedulous gain.
    When the dark apparels the sky,
    They commence to yearn and sigh
For the various shows that may lull their pain.
    Then the night glides trippingly by
In delirious joys so sterile and vain.

Ruffling with trifles, which wrap in a spell
    Their spirits from dawn till night,
    Their faces are never bright
With the glow of rapture drunk from the well
    Of Nature, whose hallowed light
May not in unfeeling regions dwell.

But engulfed in a worrying discontent
    They hunger for any joy,
    Dazzled by every toy,
However delusive, as twigs are bent
    By all breezes. Thus they destroy
Their vapid minds, grown restless and rent.

To happy solitude never incline
    Their spirits, girdled with care;
    Neither do they repair
To wandering rills that warble and shine;
    Nor can they sublimely wear
Pure bliss at Contemplation's shrine.

But hard and lonely, they run to swell
    The nearest tumultuous crowd,
    Exulting blithely in loud
And rancorous fruitlessness. Thus they quell
    Their hearts in a sordid shroud
Of follies, in which they so fondly dwell.

They tread through the vacuous ways of the world
    From their birth to their final end,
    Flaunting in swarms; they spend
Their fluttering lives in frenzy, whirled
    In fury, as bottles bend
And wallow wherever the waves are curled.

What heat envelops the stifling air!
How disgusting is this place,
Which gentle joy does not grace
With her flowery peace and ethereal fare—
Sweet Nature's inspiring face
And enamouring works that can banish care.

What serenity veils the moonlit sky,
With some stars unfolding their sheen!
Then survey this clamorous scene,
With its glare and glitter and the people who eye
The show with a staring mien,
And those distractedly hurrying by.

Better by far to erase from the mind
These sights and emerge from the roar
Into the night's kind core,
Where the ardent heart may freely unbind
Its lofty feelings and soar
To embrace fresh peace with joy entwined.

Ode to Nature

Arise and shower around your elfish gifts,
    Subtle and fresh to the exultant gaze.
Oh, Nature! Source of loving awe that lifts
      The soul, darter of the celestial rays
        Of noble wisdom, genuine knowledge, spring
      Of all ambrosial joys that flush our days;
        You, who beneath Time's arch, sublimely wing
Your eagle flight, about which shines and lies
    Eternally a great, exuberant ring
Of glory, brimmed with sternness—oh, arise!

Arise in pearly bloom and interwreathe
    Your fulgent spirit with my soul, serene
Before your hallowed being, for I breathe
      Unceasing love of you, on whom I lean
        For inspiration. So affably you shine,
      So glowingly, that I have been led to wean
        The natural fear to worship at your shrine;
Oh honey-sweet, ineffable joy to feel
    Your fairy soul so harmoniously entwines
Itself around me to uphold and heal.

From fragrant, pure recesses you distil
    An ever-fresh sublimity around,
Filling the mind with its flame, until
      It seems to shed all traces of the ground
        And float its fluent way through airy space.
      I feel my spirit soften and grow bound
        To yours, while I survey your lovely face,
Which manifold, tremendous charms suffuse
        With palpitating, most persuasive grace,
And varied, captivating, shining hues.

Oh, with what measureless wonder I behold
　　You roll forth glories, like a sumptuous dream!
With what transcendent joy I see unfold
　　Your golden harmony, lucent as a stream
　　　　Of running water; a grand purity thrills
　　From your whole frame, which ceases not to beam
　　　　Forth splashing splendours that bright beauty fills
With her celestial light—marvellous whole!
　　　　Immense, eternal as you are, in our wills
Command us to adore you with heart and soul.

Stupendous mystery! Wreathed in a coil
　　Of fathomless marvels, which flash forth and swing
Through ages their tumultuous flame, you boil
　　A wilderness of secrets. From you spring
　　　　Beauty and hue and music—whence they shoot?
　　We know not, but in vain we try to wring
　　　　For labyrinthine secrets: what the root
Of your vast being? What the colossal laws
　　　　That rule your scheme? What elements constitute
Your splendid system, which draws forth our applause?

Fresh beauty flushes through your soul and shines
　　From your veins, like the golden glow of noon.
Along your face its lambent flame reclines
　　So chaste and simple that the senses swoon
　　　　With fervour. It contains your essence, breathes
　　Into you all your value, and lies strewn
　　　　Over your scenes, as gleaming rain enwreathes
Expanses of green grass. What treasures burn
　　　　Into your pure realm—with what a group it seethes
Of beauties, which meet us at every turn.

The blissful stars that throng the heavens trill
    Cool light toward the earth; the fleet sun reels
On its diurnal round, while its rays fill
    The air with melting flame; the white moon wheels
        Along the night with frail, ethereal grace—
    How sweet to feel all these! What joy unseals
        The heart at the unfolding of the face
Of the blue sky with its soft, crystal sheen,
        To see this boundless and eternal space,
Now clothed in gold, and now a darksome scene.

The fairy clouds that fill the sky's broad floor
    Float in white fields, gilded by sunny gleams.
Mild breezes, as they flow, breathe from their core
    Their rapturous music, chanting magical dreams,
        And their cool freshness waves into the soul;
    Fleet showers fall and flash in sinuous streams,
        Weaving fine strains that fly around and roll;
The rainbow lifts its many-tinted arc;
        The dewdrops fold the greening grass, a whole
Array of pearls that cool the flowery dark.

The hills uprear their heights toward the sun,
    Their glittering tops swept over with hardy airs;
What beautiful grasses round the hill slopes run,
    Watered by rills upon which the sun glares;
        The plains unfold beneath the radiant sky
        Spaces, to which the soul for peace repairs;
        The sands gleam lightly as they roll and lie
Upon the shore, washed by rejoicing waves;
        Numberless isles sustain their beings high
Above the ocean, which restlessly raves.

In leafy woods fresh fanes of peace are found,
    Framed by long branches of the blossomy trees;
Within what fragrance reigns! The slumberous ground
    Serenely lies beneath the thrilling breeze;
        The sunny glades are clothed in lustrous green,
    The gloomy groves fling shade from which light flees;
        What sumptuous landscapes throng earth's gentle scene!
The fields lie gleaming after streams of rain,
        Or balmy with calm moonlight freely preen
Their greening herbage and their mellowing grain.

The lull of oceans and the swell of seas
    Refresh the emotions with bright joy and rest;
The sinuous blue waves bend their foam and squeeze
    Their lines with music murmuring at each crest;
        How wondrous the crystal green of lakes appears!
    To see the warm springs issuing from earth's breast,
        The ebb and flow of tides, from which uprears
A thrilling speech of joy, relieves one's pain;
        The coolness of soft rills and streams endears
Them to the heart and soothes the feverish brain.

Green trees unfold their arms and swing in sleep,
    With their light foliage waving to and fro;
What swaying fruits from the long branches peep!
    The fields of corn wriggle—a sunny show,
        Flashing and revelling underneath the sky;
    The morning plants and verdant herbage throw
        From all their pores clean redolence as they sigh;
The glimmering bloom of flowers, arrayed in hues,
        And fashioned in shapes different and spry,
Presents to us one of the happiest views.

The blithe grasshoppers warble as they hop,
    The garrulous crickets shrill in ceaseless joy;
The glow worms pour harmonious beams that drop
      With softness on the grass. The blithe and the coy
        Butterflies cling to stalks with pensile grace;
    The golden bees in the sun's warmth employ
        Their lives flying from place to flowery place;
The birds in the field and wood, in dell and hill,
      Over the sea, and in the bright cloud's face,
Chant songs that wake the heart's responsive thrill.

The fishes glide within their element
    With such bewitching motion that we stay
To watch their noiseless pace, or else, half-pent
    Within the shadowy creeks, they rest from play;
      The lovely swans on plumes of fairest hue
    Sail smoothly on, brushed by the sunset's ray;
      The squirrels leap, where peaceful shadows strew
The woody scenes, and gather dainty nuts;
      The deer in forests make a glowing view;
How gladsome to scan the cows before the huts!

What varied hues clothe your enamouring scene!
    The green of leaves, and the blue of sky and waves,
The white of clouds are those you preen,
    In whose enticing balm the spirit laves;
      Sweet are the rose of sunrise, gold of noon,
    And the pure purple from the sunset's caves;
      The lights that wake, and shades that cause to swoon
The woods and skies, entwine their joyous play;
      The innumerable colours that lie strewn
Over the flowers and birds are fine and gay.

Most dulcet sounds fall on the ruptured soul,
    The blithe tunes poured through leaves as through a sieve;
The subtle purl of blissful streams that roll,
    And flowing rain, the songs that breezes weave,
        And the live music floating from the seas;
    The lapping of the waves that rock and heave;
        The slumberous hum of swarms of peaceful bees;
The thrilling tones of insects among the grass;
        The singing of the birds, perched on the trees,
Upon the wing, or as they upward pass.

The softness of the flowers and luscious fruits,
    The coolness of the water and the air,
The freshness of fine fountains and green shoots,
    And murmuring brooks, and morning, which lay bare
        Showers of gentle winds and twinkling dews;
    The delicate warmth, which flushes attractive, fair
        Days, and the tender radiance, which imbues
Purpureal evenings and moonlight nights;
        The shining smoothness that on leaves one views—
How pleasant to feel all these great delights!

The ambrosial taste of fruit is strongly sweet;
    Pure water soothes the sense deliciously;
The fragrance breathed from flowers makes the brain beat,
    Intoxicated with delirious glee;
        The odours flung by gales give freshest joy—
    All these throng your sublime fertility;
        And glories, such as these—which can rebuoy
The soul with a clear pleasure and pure love
        Of their fine beauty that has no alloy
Of baser metal—over such we rove.

But oh! strange Nature, in your mighty realm,
     Such a tremendous violence also reigns,
That with full fury it can overwhelm,
     When its lithe force is loosened from its chains,
          The brain with ardour as to make it reel—
     What flaming objects flow from out your veins,
          On which the gaze dwells with enamoured zeal,
Feeling no satisfaction of such food.
          A vision of these makes the spirit feel
Enlarged and raised to an aspiring mood.

The burning furnace of the noontide sun,
     Sweeping its scorching rays onto the earth;
The pouring rains that make the day so dun,
     Rushing from out the clouds, their place of birth;
          The sombre skies clothed in appalling gloom;
     Fierce tempests and swift hurricanes that girth
          The globe, in land or sea, and wildly boom;
The whirling rivers, winding endlessly
          Towards the deep to fall within this room—
What violence fills them to eternity!

What stormy beauties roll into the view!
     Sinuous winds that sing in a wild tone;
The lightning, flashing out its golden hue
     And wreathing the dark sky as with a zone;
          The thunder that now grumbles and then roars,
     And then it trembles off with murmuring groan;
          The lowering clouds that run their pathless course
To shelter from the sight the shadowy sky;
          The surges lashing the engirding shores
With stirring fury as they swiftly fly.

Behold the mountains with their lofty crowns,
    So grand and wonderful in all their stark
Simplicity, the rocks, whose threatening frowns
    Hover in tremulous fashion over dark,
        Tumultuous waves that boil and glow beneath;
    And the profound ravines where scarce a spark
        Of light is found—where rivers ever seethe
And proudly roar; the forests framed in gloom,
        Swarming with myriad lives that roam and breathe,
And with wild flowers and trees in glorious bloom.

The deserts spread their endless miles of sand
    Beneath the skies; the wildernesses run
Their barren length; the precipices stand
    In solemn solitude; the caves from dun
        And shadowy mouths pour sparkling waters out;
    The cataracts, exulting fiercely, stun
        The ear, as they leap down the rocks and shout;
The oceans sweep around the desolate shores,
        Churning the water, while their ceaseless rout
Of raving waves uplift their frightful roars.

What monstrous terrors hold their hideous sway!
    The mad volcanoes hurl their smoke and flame
Towards the skies; the portentous earthquakes play
    Upon the world and rock its solid frame
        In feeble spots with great, destructive ire;
    Floods overflow the riverbanks and claim
        The land around, and then they slowly tire
After their ruining sweep, and thus assuage;
        The forest flames that roar and soar with dire
Intent demolish much to glut their rage.

The terrible animals of every kind
    Horribly prowl in forests that they keep:
Enormous fishes cleave their paths and find
    Their dwelling place within the stormy deep,
        And there in lonely grandeur they abide;
    The hideous serpents, while they lie or creep,
        Watch with invincible vigilance to slide
Their fangs into their foes; the birds of prey
        Suddenly swoop from trees towards the side
Of their small brethren that wing past their way.

What ugly things are also to be found!
    The vultures go wherever carrion lies
Waiting to be devoured; upon the ground
    The scorpions lurk in slumbering disguise,
        Waiting to sting those who come past by chance;
    The spiders wait to prey on hapless flies,
        Sitting amid their silken webs, which dance
And glitter in the sun; the ugly toads
        Creep in damp ways; the lizards quickly glance
Past up the trees or on grass-covered roads

With beauty and with terror intertwined
    To raise or daunt the heart—within your clime
What objects breathe! Oh you!—in space enshrined
    And rolling in the stream of ceaseless time.
        For all the glories that enthral the soul
    I lift my utmost praise, for the sublime
        Symmetry of the parts, which form your whole!
Oh, breathe on me divinest happiness,
        Enchanting me, reading the ample scroll
Of mighty works, spread round in bright excess.

Unceasing change enfolds the various forms
    That shine in your vast pageant, and that quake
With an intense emotion and with storms
    Of such tumultuous bliss, we must awake
        The spirit to respond with radiant joy.
    None of your fairest beauties do not make
        New changes with swift time, which must destroy
All things, ugly or fair, and then create
        Afresh the new—ephemeral too—which buoy
Themselves up, but to founder soon or late.

What numerous labyrinths of laws entwine
    Themselves around your frame! Such mighty laws
So hard to understand, to let them shine
    Full on our minds, and know the effect and cause
        Of each of the great glories that we see.
    In strong sublimity arrayed, they pause
        A marvellous band from all eternity,
Within whose stern and forceful bounds we live,
        Not to be broken if we would be free
From undesirable woes that you can give.

A universal order you can show.
    Its every part to every other part
Is linked to form a scheme we scarcely know,
    But which we reverence from the very heart,
        Though we but faintly trace your balanced form.
    A certain unity is found to dart
        From all your complex qualities that storm
Through countless ages in wild majesty—
        What harmony can be more exalted, more warm?
What better symmetry can our dreams set free?

You swing through time fulfilling your own end,
    Running along with rushing energy;
What is the splendid fate whereto you tend
    With such high eagerness? What destiny
        Is bound up with your strange, colossal frame?
    Through all your roll in great eternity,
        What works of glory, clothed in thundering flame
Have burst forth to adorn you for a while,
        Then to return to whence they at first came?
What is the meaning of this restless toil?

Tremendous Nature! From you we can learn
    The true and sweet and free and happy life;
You shower upon us from your healing urn
    Celestial balm to soothe our mental strife,
        And you pile dizzy raptures on the soul:
    Oh, let your kingdom be for ever rife
        With such stupendous glories as may roll
In land or sea or air to charm the heart!
        Wherever I may wander, let me stroll
Through daedal scenes of such miraculous art.

Peace

In my bosom such peace reclines
    As arises but seldom in me;
What rhythmic content intertwines
      Lush tendrils of joy and repose!
    Oh, the marvellous harmony
Of my soul with great Nature, which shines
      So serenely around that all woes
    In the world seem unable to be!
      Through my spirit what freshness flows!

My unruffled condition of soul
    Is as soothing as shimmering waves,
Which sing sunny songs as they roll
      In their depth of ephemeral bliss.
    How complete is the calm that paves
All the space in my being's scroll!
      I inhale a blitheness that is
    So exuberant all the caves
      Of joy seem to pour on me this.

A stupendous feeling of rest
    Pervades all my rapturous frame,
Thus enabling my mind to invest
      Itself with the power to view
    All the world with a steadier flame;
I can taste with a happier zest
      All the wonders that Nature can strew
    In her realm—both the wild and the tame;
      Peace sparkles like flourishing dew.

I feel as if wrapped in a dream
    While I have such a tranquil mood;
From my brain enchantingly beam
        Strange fancies and thoughts that arise
    In continual waves—I can brood
On the future with bliss, and I teem
        With hopes that are bright like the skies;
    I can think there may still be some good
        To befall me that I would prize.

While surveying the scene around
    Peace subtly arises in me;
All the earth and the heavens are bound
        By a girdle of glorious calm.
    The unparalleled harmony
That pervades all the air has wound
        About me its odorous balm;
    This enamouring purity
        Has flung from me every qualm.

What a freshness flows from the wings
    Of the breeze, inhaling the scent
Of the flowers; how blithely it sings
        In its sinuous flow through this wood.
    On the clouds and the firmament
The hues from the sun's full springs
        Flash softly. The birds in a mood
    Of mellifluous, joyous content,
        With their songs wrap this solitude.

Such a subtle influence has
　　This scene on the soul that I seem
To melt into the magical mass
　　　　Of aerial glories around.
　　My spirit assumes a gleam
Of something ennobling. I pass
　　　　Through sensations so strange they astound
　　My brain, urging I am in a dream.
　　　　What a wonderful peace have I found!

What delicious tranquillity here
　　Sublimely diffuses divine
Enchantment and joy to uprear
　　　　The spirit with firmness and hope;
　　The sweet music and glitter combine
To charm both the eye and the ear;
　　　　I ascend with rapture the slope
　　Of serene contemplation. I shine
　　　　With calmness, like evening's cope.

To Fire

The showery songs you fashion forth bequeath
    The sternest joy to me,
From the aerial lisps you blithely breathe
    To awful roars you free
    From out your flaming sea.

From your tumultuous heart those tunes arise
    And, floating on fleet wings,
They ripple into mine and realise
    For me such joy as sings
    In your ethereal springs.

What lucent beauty round your boiling waves
    Hovers in lambent dance,
And what fine rapture girdles you and laves
    Your liquid countenance
    In a soft radiance!

Your flashing splendour brushes with smooth gold
    All things within your gaze,
And their gloom rolls away when you enfold
    Their forms with arrowy rays,
    Which glide from out your blaze.

Grand is the pageant that, in stern unrest,
    Your leaping tongues sustain;
Now they blend, playing wildly on your breast—
    And now they part again,
    Like waves upon the main.

In all directions and in ceaseless streams
    Heat flows from your soft sea,
And the air fills with it, while my frame teems
    With warmth, which brushes me
    Very deliciously.

Your ardour enters my responsive heart
    And makes it beat and flame
In sympathy with you, and tempests dart
    About it, till the same
    Joy as yours wreathes its frame.

When I behold you play your endless whims,
    Bewitching reveries
Awake within my mind, which overbrims
    With them and cannot cease
    To hear their melodies.

On Weariness

The sea in momentary delight
    Gleams for a while with smiles,
But weary soon its bright,
    Lyrical face is furrowed with files
    Of waves and overboils.

A glow worm, shining in its wet seat
    Of grass, reposes and dreams
Amid its lucent heat;
    But lulled by descending, dewy streams,
    At last it closes its beams.

A bird in a swift, Daedalian flight
    Exultingly surveys
The serene, enchanting sight;
    Then tired it ceases its wandering ways,
    And within its nest it stays.

But weariness only for a time
    Engirdles their spirit. Again
They will soon be free from their lime.
    But, alas, it wreathes with a rigorous chain
    My entire revolving brain!

I feel the pulse of life and the world
    Throb wearily to and fro;
The pinions of joy are furled;
    And all—adrift in destruction—go,
    Replete with perennial woe.

My soul with its bloomless foliage reels
    Knowing not where to turn
For refreshing solace. It feels
    How sterile it is to pant and yearn
    For any star that may burn.

Ah! Vain is the ruining toil we bear,
 Hunting enamouring bliss!
And ah! How rankling to wear
 In our spirits the dreams we are bound to miss!
 Ah! How oppressive it is!

The hopes that we nourished dwindle away,
 Bequeathing only despair.
And the night succeeds the day;
 And our ponderous hearts become a lair,
 Which passionate scorpions tear.

Alas! That peace is so hard to obtain,
 And I can only mourn
That such wild unrest and pain
 Have trammelled me long, and still rage and burn,
 While joy does not return.

Doubt

While we thrill to the supreme
   Marvel, Nature's universal
   Frame, we must immerse all
Thoughts in the labyrinthine stream
Of hard speculation on this lofty theme.

But our finespun theories soon
   Like soft stones dissolve and crumble,
   Leaving us to grope and fumble
Once anew by the dim moon
Of our intellect—a harsh, tormenting boon.

The laborious coils we weave
   To enwind our minds, like tapers,
   Are soon clouded with thick vapours;
Still we ever will believe
That life's secret is such as we can perceive.

All the things that we behold
   Seem to flow like dreams around us,
   Serving only to confound us
With their strangeness; to unfold
Their deep mystery is as difficult as of old.

Why, our very hopes are faint—
   Hopes that float on broken pinions;
   And our thoughts are not the minions
Of great truth, which does but paint
On our minds delusive hues without restraint.

To what end do we exist?
    What was the sublime beginning
    Of the universe, whose spinning
Is enfolded in a mist?
Its dark secret is hard as a knotty twist.

What is Nature's ultimate goal
    To which she so serenely rushes?
    What means life with all its flushes
Of pure joy, and griefs that roll
Ceaselessly, and sharp strife written on the scroll?

When I view a flashing star,
    A bird soaring in the distance,
    Or a flower in fresh existence,
Bursting with surprise, I war
With myself in trying to know why they are.

Ah! But when my spirit soars,
    Just to grasp these many questions,
    Which shed showers of unrest once
They arouse our wonder—their roars
Scare it back from those dark, unapproachable shores.

Hard it must be to discern
    That any central thread extending
    Through the whole—can we be wending
Towards knowledge, when we turn
Even from conceiving its size, so vast and stern?

Thus, our life is churned away
    In a whirling doubt that wearies
    Us, while seldom ever varies
Care its torture day to day—
Our firm cause is lost, and aimlessly we stray.

I am borne along the stream
    Of tumultuous life, while leaning
    On no hope that any meaning
Of the universe can beam
On our knowledge, dubious like a flickering beam.

Sinking underneath a load
    Of colossal strife and trouble,
    I can find no joys to bubble
In my heart—Despair's abode—
But must journey on in the same restless mood.

Beneath a Tree

The sun is gently slanting through the leaves,
    Continual roll of clouds on high arise,
    Unfolding burnished white, the rapturous skies
Gleam blue between these sunny sheets and sheaves;
Beneath the shade, which this benign tree weaves,
    I sit and see the scene in beauteous guise
    Spread round me, feeling my soul harmonize
With it, to which a subtle stillness cleaves;
Blithe breezes creep about with lingering grace,
    Lavishing fancies on the lonely ear,
And, as these sportive wonders mildly race
Along, they breathe their coolness on the face;
    I find a mellow, impressive silence here,
And wish it may ever rest in this place.

To the Sky

Wonderful vault! Expanse of blue that lies
    In limpid, elfish beauty, brushed with flame
    From the flush furnace flourishing in your frame,
And gazing down with burning, arrowy eyes;
Ocean where nestle jewels, which arise
    At night to adorn your slumberous face and claim
    Devoted homage—the moon showering shame
Upon the dark, the stars that time despises.
Whenever I behold your brow display
    Its depth of beaming bliss and dreamy calm,
Though in my heavy spirit not a ray
Of joy remains but care makes me its prey,
    You shed on my sad mind mysterious balm
And fill my heart with cool peace, soft as spray.

The Nocturnal Wanderer

Tranquillest gloom enmeshed the sky above.
　　Only a few faint, failing stars, dispersed
　　At spacious intervals, rolled forth and burst
With dolorous light to view, and, like a dove,
　　　　The crescent moon endeavoured to unbind
The expansive mass of dreary clouds that wove
　　　　A screen around the cope and show its kind,
　　Though spiritless rays; the chilly air was still.
　　Only such silent darkness breathed its fill
　　　　As casts a shade upon the blithest mind.

Deserted and dark dozed the winding road,
　　Which, wrapped in slumber, wreathed its lengthy course
　　On which, as if impelled along by force,
Only a solitary figure strode,
　　　　Apparently oblivious of his way;
At times to behold the peaceful moon, which rode
　　　　Dimly along, he raised his face to pay
　　Restless attention to the shadowy scene
　　Painted upon the sky, whose weary sheen
　　　　Appeared to lure him with its gentle play.

As he emerged into the wavering light
　　Of one of the infrequent lamps, which hung
　　Over the lonely road and softly flung
Its dancing locks on the desponding night,
　　　　Could be beheld the turbulent countenance
Of a young man endeavouring with great might
　　　　To still some inward tremulous mischance.
　　His agitated motion and his brow,
　　So stern and gloomy, indicated how
　　　　Deeply his soul was pricked by sorrow's lance.

Why did he walk with a wild, faltering gait,
  Wandering forth in a delirious way?
  What made him at this weary hour stray
Into the uninviting night so late?
    What fiery scourges made him look severe,
Despairingly gazing on the desolate
    Darkness with a pale face so worn and drear?
  How great the wound must be within his brain
  That made his visage thus convulse with pain,
    And printed on it lines so deep and sere!

His father was a prosperous merchant—his
  People for generations were engaged
  In trade—in their coarse spirits always raged
Only the love of gain—a glorious bliss!
    His neighbours all were framed in the same mould.
No softer dream of happiness than this—
    This ceaseless and absorbing pursuit of gold—
  Ever by any chance disturbed their days;
  The man, who won their most untiring praise,
    Was he with greatest wealth within his hold.

Amid such marshy pools his youthful mind
  Struggled for light. From boyhood he soon grew
  To be indifferent to the talk, which blew
Among his neighbours. Not the least inclined
    Towards bright wealth, he did not feel the call
Of solemn, shallow trade, which could not bind
    His spirit. Vaguely he felt the weary thrall
  Of living underneath its influence
  Within this wilderness of misery. Hence
    Aversion slowly wrapped him with its pall.

He had deep feelings and a passionate soul,
    But these were latent. To the cursory view
    His nature was endowed with none or few
Qualities marking him out from the roll
        Of common boys; as yet he had no need
To keep his embryo storms beneath control;
        In perfect peace he dwelt and paid no heed
    To ordinary things; in reverie
    Wont to indulge, as happy as a bee,
        He made his days glide on with dreaming speed.

He was engirdled with a wide, keen love
    Of nature and found spiritual food
    In great profusion in a sea or wood,
In the meandering fish or glossy dove;
        He loved to roam alone on the wild shore
And to behold the spacious sky above;
        He found that he could open nature's door
    And wondered at the beauties there displayed,
    Feeling serene content beneath the shade
        Of trees, where he could rustle reverie's store.

He saw the sky alight on the earth, concealed
    In a pool of water, with adoring joy;
    Aerial blitheness never failed to buoy
His spirit, when—depressed awhile—he appealed
        For consolation to the gorgeous show
Of flowers; the clouds, which formed a shimmering shield
        On the sky, soothed him with their tinted glow;
    In the repose of gentle nature's lap
    He passed his years; the colour and the flap
        Of foliage ran in his life's ebb and flow.

Manhood attained, his family introduced
  Him into the resplendent realm of trade;
  Though little to his liking, he yet paid
Close heed to its details and was soon fused
   Into a quite respectable merchant, but
Though victory crowned his efforts, though quite used
   To his condition—impossible to cut
  One's instincts handed downwards from of old
  Completely off—aversion still laid hold
   On him at times to life within this rut.

The coarse vulgarity of the men he met—
  Fardels of fuss—in daily intercourse.
  The enthralling spell of futile trade—the source
Of petty wrangling and a brawling set
   Of flourishing ills too numerous to name.
All the world trying to besiege and net
   Up anything that came along—a game
  Of rivalry. People with their thoughts bent
  On trade alone. All these harassed and rent
   His peace with a destructive maze of flame.

The incessant and torrential ebb and flow
  Of streets—rivers of evil—with their huge
  Swarms hurrying up and down in a deluge
Of reeling restlessness, which makes them go
   Through life, untouched by sweet serenity's dew
The hoarse, resounding cries, uplifted so
   Intense and overwhelming, which imbue
  The dusty air—the men, completely whirled
  In a wild maelstrom of desires—this world
   Is utterly repellent in his view.

For several years he worked at a hot pace,
    With approbation from his kith and kin;
    He toiled industriously amid the din
And dust of business, trying to erase
        Any disdain with which he was instilled
Towards the venomous pursuit of base,
        Pernicious gain; his hopeful heart was filled
    With tolerable peace; of caustic care,
    Which rends with fury, he had nought to bear;
        But though repressed his aversion was not killed.

The strength of his slow-gathering disgust,
    Which had been kept within controlling bounds,
    And only trembled with soft, haunting sounds
Within him fitfully at times, now thrust
        Its glittering rapier through his anguished mind,
And swept through him like a tumultuous gust—
        A fiery, stormy, unimprisoned wind;
    His spirit was transformed and swiftly fell
    Beneath chaotic tumult's trenchant spell,
        Any escape from which he could not find.

His weariness of commerce had now reached
    Its limit, and no longer could he bear
    Its influence. The dark vultures of despair
Gnawed at his bitter heart and shrilly screeched
        As helplessly he sat within his place
Of trade that day. His mind could not be bleached
        Of the dark hues of misery. The face
    Of dull, depressing gloom was always turned
    Towards his view. Such fiery anguish burned,
        As made joy quite depart, leaving no trace.

At close of evening he departed home;
    But his sad fate continued to pursue
    Him with persistent force—a clamouring crew
Of gloomy thoughts, like stormy clouds that roam
        Across the sky, tinged with no hint of gold,
Or wrecks, which toss upon the ocean's foam;
        His fancy was unable to unfold
    Any bright image, but a single chain
    Of ideas, interwoven with deep pain,
        Grasped him with a voracious spider's hold.

Unable to endure the violence
    Of his thoughts any longer, he arose,
    And, seeking peace, he entered a wood, close
To his abode. The tall trees breathed a sense
        Of joy and trilled fine notes along the air
From their vivacious guests, shooting intense
        Rapturous life—the flowers, delicious fare!
    Heralds of peace with soft grace floated down
    And, lying beneath his feet, profusely thrown
        Over the ground, serenely glimmered there.

The vocal winds stirred gently, lavishing meet,
    Sinuous songs; the evening sun lay red,
    Slanting through the resplendent wood, and shed
Its gracious rays; the heavens shone a sheet
        Of rose and white and blue; the golden bees
Hummed happily as they flew about to greet
        Each other, preparing to desert the seas
    Of luminous blossoms; hopping among the grass,
    The chirping elves were garrulous of the mass
        Of verdurous herbage and the soothing breeze.

The brook ran gurgling underneath his feet,
    Merrily murmuring a sunny tale—
    Unquenchable eloquence. It did not fail
To keep a countenance so serene and sweet
        Every dimple showed its benignant joy;
Some golden cassia, blossoms on its neat,
        Crystalline bosom, floated in a coy
    And gentle fashion; the mellifluous stream
    Breathed peace and happiness, as in a dream—
Happiness mingled with no sad alloy.

Peace reigned around him, but he could not feel
    As usual any joy in the dulcet scene.
    Such injuries chaotic tumult's keen
Dagger had worked that it could neither heal
        Nor touch his spirit—warped by torturing hate.
Instead on it was stamped the glacial seal
        Of trade. The enfolding misery of his state,
    Try as he might, he could not disarray:
    He trembled restlessly—a tragic prey
        Within the coils of his unfortunate fate.

Soon the sun glided down and gloom unrolled
    Its slumberous wings, with scattered stars enlaced;
    Deep in reflection he at random traced
His steps towards the town, which could unfold
        To him no vestige of a soothing smile.
His spirit filled with tumult as he strolled
        Along the streets, viewing the shops, where guile
    Mingled with fuss, and the vociferous streams
    Of people muffled in pernicious dreams;
        Amid these waves he glowed a lonely isle.

He rambled in the town till night was late;
      The shops had breathed their work's diurnal close,
      And all had wrapped themselves in sweet repose;
Silently he propelled his weary gait
      Towards his home in a mechanical way;
As if beneath the influence of fate,
      Wholly unconscious of the things that lay
      Around his path, he journeyed in a dream,
      Filled with revolt against life's ills—no gleam
Of comfort lulling his tempestuous day.

He paced along in his volcanic mood,
      Enwound within the mesh of bitter thoughts;
      The cold, remorseless night from dusky grots
Revealed the weary stars in heaven's hood,
      Shooting faint light in soft, serene repose;
The moon, with pale and slumberous visage, stood
      Behind the clouds, regardless of his woes,
      Anxious to cease its dull, laborious flight;
      Shedding no sympathy the swarthy night
Hovered a phantom, nebulous, stern, morose.

A gentle wind arose and drowsily moaned
      Its pensive tune—a spirit in the night,
      Wandering and repeating in its flight
Its shy, nocturnal dreams. The tall trees frowned
      On either side of the road in quiet sleep,
And scarcely waved their pendent boughs or droned
      Forth any note. The birds had ceased to sweep
      The air or chirp. All nature softly fell
      To sleep, while he was muffled by the spell
Of anguish, which had never ceased to keep.

Ah! What a curse it is to be alone
    On a dark road wrapped in tempestuous waves
    Of thought, with the dun mystery night engraves
Upon the heart. The vast and fathomless zone
        Of darkness serves to fill the mental frame
With deeper gloom. When weariness lies prone
        In balmy slumber, when the restless aim
    Of life releases its tentacular grasp,
    The lonely wanderer's thoughts are sure to clasp
        No gemmy brightness—no soft, flowery flame.

As he, without regard to flowing time,
    Journeyed on restless as a buzzing bee,
    Feverish thoughts swept through the stormy sea
Created by his brain—thoughts of the grime,
        The manifest vulgarity of life;
Up its steep slope of rocks we wearily climb,
        Spending our days in bitter, endless strife;
    We dawdle along, bereft of all true good,
    Our spirits wallowing in repulsive food,
        In cavernous gloom where passions and pain are rife.

Within his soul he passionately cried—
    What is this wearisome existence for?
    That one should strive with all his might and roar
Through the long day, completely steeped and dyed
        In the dark stream of feverish chase of joy?
Now vain it is to run from side to side,
        Trying to grasp the rose of pleasure, coy
    And tenderly frail to such a great degree,
    That when we light on it and think we see
        It in our grasp, it breaks—a broken toy.

Drearily we are borne on sorrowing wings.
 Alas! Where are we hurrying forward then?
 We stray about and live within the den
Of the bleak world, which gives no joy but brings
  Only disgust and dark, corrosive grief;
Naught in our spirits glimmers, full of stings
  And darkness, fringed with a surrounding reef
 Of dreams, through which we may not try to sweep;
 On our dark night no rosy dawn can peep
  For any length, but shrivels like a leaf.

Ah! Why should men their lives to hideous trade
 Wholly consign with all their breath and flame?
 Why should they go and unconscionably maim
Their souls beyond repair and let them fade
  To a dull texture? Voracious birds of prey
They live, forever ready to make a raid
  On everything that hovers past their way:
 They wish for nothing else but to amass
 Destructive heaps of sordid, useless brass,
  Working incessantly day after day.

They walk along the road without green grass,
 Beneath the sky where no bright sunlight smiles,
 A joyous sheet of glorious gold, where piles
No cloud its wavy, shining, silvery mass;
  No winsome breaths refresh their weary way;
But fast entwined in the world's coils, alas!
  Their lives are seas of care naught can allay;
 Their spirits are devoid of the soft flame
 Of peace, which only on minds of virtuous frame
  Is found to cast its bright, enamouring ray.

Wrapped in such thoughts he wildly walked along
　　With fierce, delirious tumult, racking pain,
　　Trembling and thundering in his fevered brain,
Continuously creating a dark throng
　　　　Of thoughts, like whirling waters in the sea.
The tempest in his helpless soul with strong,
　　　　Persistent sweep, raged angrily and set free
　　Its terrifying, destructive force. He knew
　　All blazing agonies of the brain, due
　　　　To thoughts let out by fell reflection's key.

Life had become unbearable to him;
　　From it had gone whatever golden light
　　That could cheer him with its sustaining might;
A sheet of cloudy foam—so cold and dim—
　　　　Enwreathed his soul and paralysed his breast;
Life's cup was filled with bitterness to the brim;
　　　　He could not give his spirit tranquil rest;
　　All dreams had vanished into empty air;
　　On the bleak tree of violent despair
　　　　The clamorous hurricane rocked his flimsy nest.

Continuing his walk, at last he came
　　By chance to a wild place and made his way
　　To a dark river, of small extent, which lay
On the outskirts of the town; it bared its frame
　　　　To the smooth slumber of the vaulted sky;
It seemed to wander along without an aim,
　　　　Drearily chanting a soft elegy;
　　The chilly night poured down its streams of dew
　　On the dank, fringing grass of verdant hue,
　　　　Which grew around in great fertility.

The winding river beckoned with eager hands,
　　Inviting him into its cold embrace.
　　The floating ripples danced with gloomy face,
Binding his spirit as with iron bands.
　　　　The garrulous waters seemed to rise and cleave
To him and draw him down with magic wands.
　　　　The plaintive, persistent murmurs seemed to weave
　　Around him the soft spell of a siren song,
　　As he thus lingered over the dark throng
　　　　Of waves, from which he could not take his leave.

At last on an impulsive thought, which took
　　Entire possession of his giddy brain,
　　He jumped into the river, which had lain
In wait for him with a caressing look;
　　　　Like a sweet lullaby it gently breathed
A mournful song, and its dark waters shook
　　　　With such light motion that the soul that seethed
　　With anguished tumult slumbered in supreme
　　Serenity, and realised its dream
　　　　Of rest, with which it was at length enwreathed.

The Butterfly

On that green orchid stalk the butterfly
    Perches in dreaming bliss and bland repose,
    While the bright sun upon its body throws
Kind rays, which make it gleam so gloriously;
But it soon rises from its seat with spry,
    Ethereal grace when the breeze sings and blows,
    And, revelling in this coolness, blithely flows
Wherever fancy lures its liberty.
Oh! What a wonderful life it must enjoy,
    Without a fringe of care, without a pain;
    It glides along one smooth, continuous chain
Of sunny happiness that cannot cloy,
    Now slumbering on the flowers, and now again
Upon the wing—a soft, aerial buoy.

To a Glow Worm

Oh, glimmering gem of the balmy gloom!
    Nestling among the grass in the shade,
You are pillowed in the ambrosial bloom
Of peace, while you gloriously illume
    With that chill jewel—your flame—the blade,
On which you repose—your grassy room.

Encumbered with genial drops of dew,
    The grass is blowing with sweetness and joy,
And it thrills to the breezes, which imbue
Its leaves with the odorous green of their hue,
    And which rill around, expanding their coy,
Fresh wings, and coolness abundantly strew.

The world is completely enmeshed by sleep,
    And enamouring silence reigns around,
Save the breezes, from which serenely creep
Canorous tunes, and the crickets, which keep
    Their garrulous song up with merry sound,
Which serves but to make the stillness deep.

The pensile stars from their chinks in the sky
    Flash softly, gemming the face of the night,
Breathing celestial calm from their shy,
Aerial winks; there dark clouds try
    To conceal the moon, whose shadowy light
At intervals shimmers to the eye.

Carelessly pressing your leaf in ease
    And dreaming superbly in tender delight,
You grow lightly lulled by the brushing breeze;
You peruse the scene and brood over these
    Verdurous glories, wrapped in bright,
Mellifluous thoughts, I fain would seize.

Your life is goaded by no fell sting,
　　But lying contentedly you shine
And your golden, enamouring light you fling
Around, thus weaving a luminous ring
　　Of hue, like that of those stars, so divine
And chaste, which shoot down their rays on the wing.

The peace you diffuse within this zone
　　Smoothly girdles all things and floats
Into my heart, whose gloom has flown—
Peace, which is slowly instilled and blown
　　Upon the responsive breast, whose notes
Of bitterness soon are overthrown.

Your gentleness makes me loath to turn
　　Away, oh lucent atom of fire!
But to linger and continue to learn
Of you the rearing of peace, and I mourn
　　That you cannot fulfil my earnest desire
That you perennially may burn.

The Distant Prospect

In showers from the sluice of heaven flow
    The glittering beams with swift, propitious pace;
    They fill and nestle against the spacious place
Above the azure heaven's brim, where blow
    Soft breezes; with what delicate beauty race
The golden glories!—with what fervour glow,
    Brushing with splendour the cope's blissful face.

They burn the shoals of billowy clouds, which lie
    In floating ease into aerial joys,
    Which storms or rains ought not to mar—such buoys
Of dreamy glory!—but should ever fly
    Far, far away! Every piece employs
Itself in frolicsome play! Can anything vie
    With their bright splendour! Can vain human toys?

Lo! Here a woolly phalanx gently spreads
    Its shameless mass—the languishing expanse,
    Which tenderly shines with a white countenance,
Rippling inaudibly—and there faint shreds,
    And downy curls, in flimsy beauty, dance,
Winnowed by noiseless airs; but their frail threads
    Of life soon snap—they die off in a trance.

Like sable shadows flecking the cope's face,
    A numerous flock of birds with arrowy flight,
    In close formation, suddenly to sight
Upspring, and, gliding with incredible grace,
    Soar in magnificent earnestness—the light
Giving them joy—but their united race
    Is now dissolved: they scatter left and right.

Some finely skim with smoothly-swaying glide,
    With the sun shining on their glittering wings,
    Floating about in fleet and rapturous rings;
While others shoot or dip from side to side,
    Having no scheme, but such as fancy brings;
Gently and lightly here and there they ride
    Along, profoundly drinking from joy's springs.

Over there what serenity must repose.
    No note of sadness sullies the expanse,
    Whose splendid, harmonizing hues entrance
The eye and free the mind from heavy woes;
    What joy is written on its countenance,
Diffusing balm around, which gently flows
    Into all things! How bright is its clear glance!

To lie upon this fresh, green field and dream
    Beneath the shade of this embowering tree,
    Surrounded by fresh airs, which float in glee,
Upon the thronging glories there, which beam
    Forth such alluring beauty, is to free
The mind from its great gloom, while sweet thoughts teem
    In it, as if unlocked by a golden key.

Alas! That ceaseless, agitating strife
    Is ours and noisy tumult is our chain,
    Unlike the peaceful scene, which fills with pain
And wounds the feeling breast with the sharp knife
    Of deep regret, when we compare that plain
Of happy calm with the obstreperous life
    We lead—so full of misery and so vain.

While such enamouring bliss pervades that spot
    And all those things are clothed with clear repose,
    We are tossed in a whirlwind of dark woes,
Which poison and make sad our finest thought;
    Our path is strewn with broken dreams, which rose
Awhile to be with earnest ardour sought
    After by us, and then sink down and close.

We spend our life in forging link by link
    Of a delirious chain of restlessness,
    Which strives to bind in bondage and oppress
Our souls; although we zealously may shrink
    From such a fearful gulf of dark distress,
Yet we will fall into it soon and sink:
    Our brains may not be free from it the less!

Then round our brows a deep fatigue declines
    And the fragrant flowers of joy within us fade,
    And we perforce must linger in the shade
On which the sun of happiness hardly shines.
    When our unceasing mental strife has stayed
Its course, we find a weariness entwines
    Itself around our hearts, which stand dismayed.

But the kind scene before me is so sweet
    That let me snatch a momentary wave
Of bliss, like light that floats into a cave,
    And let it with its soothing beauty cheat
My mind of its sad thoughts and softly lave
    My spirit, while I see the clear, blue sheet
    Of sky fine light and cloudy glories pave.

Curious

The myriads of ephemeral schemes
 The populous brain conceives
Are frail as gossamery dreams,
 Which soft sleep subtly weaves;
Fortune with all her shades and beams
 Dispenses them like leaves.

He, who for some blithe children yearns,
 May ever long in vain;
For him, whose daily labour earns
 A title with toil and pain,
Year after endless year returns
 With babies in her train.

A man of forty odd and frail
 In health about a year,
Seized with the notion that his tale
 Of days would disappear
Soon, and desiring not to fail
 Ere end of life's career,

To wreathe his time with bliss and glee,
 Squandered his wealth, and then
He lived in utmost penury
 Till three score years and ten,
Cursing his stars, he could not see
 The fate that governs men.

From the most trifling incident
    Dire troubles may begin;
A man was singing as he went,
    When on a banana skin
He slipped, and due to that event
    He bore a broken shin.

Oh! Many are the caddish tricks
    That fickle Fortune plays;
We never would endure her kicks
    If we only knew her ways,
Although this good she gives, her pricks
    Diversify our days.

In a Town

What elfish beauty fills the silent night!
　Through the extensive firmament's small cells
Innumerable stars flash forth their white,
　　　Flourishing flowers and wink their sleepless eyes,
　　Enchanting the stern gloom with fulgent spells;
　　　Some, set like jewels, lavish lonely light,
Some hang in social groups and fraternize,
　　While some—exuberant pleasure sweeps and swells
　　　Their spirits—faint away like lingering sighs.

The viewless fabric of the genial air
　Enfolds the slumberous earth; mild breezes blow;
They rise and vanish stealthily; and where,
　　　Where is there anything else as fresh and fine
　　As these nocturnal wanderers, which throw
Around their rills? What softest faces wear
　　　The shadowy, tall angsana trees, which line
　The streets! No audible sound—however low—
　　　Upsprings. Even the birds no longer whine.

The staggering silence is ineffably deep—
　Impressive—and more stunning to the mind
Than noise. An oppressive feeling seems to creep
　　　Over me as I view the town, so still
　　That not a murmur ripples through the rind
Of peace embowering it. Profoundest sleep
　　　Enmeshes all. No human voices rill
　Upon the balmy night in which enshrined
　　　Lies rest, as soft as the fresh dews that trill.

I am alone beneath this lamp that throws
    Refulgent rays around; within this place
People abound. Yet to me solitude shows
        Her sternest aspect—why? To be awake
    Amid a sleeping town is to embrace
        The heaviest loneliness. Self-conscious grows
The mind of it. But, when apart, to make
    The spirit blithe, content, one needs must face
        Only plain nature; thus life's ills best slake.

Now veils repose all men beneath its wings.
    Weary, they rest from their perennial stir,
Their feverish hurry, their distracted rings
        Of hopes and cares. Perforce relinquished now
    From the colossal trifles, they defer
        Only a slumbering while, such rapturous things
Will they—freshened—embrace tomorrow. How
    Zealously they will toil, as though they were
        Chasing the noblest aim that life can show.

What a repulsive spectacle the day
    Will soon unfold. How can it otherwise seem—
With its delirious tumult and display
        Of clamouring crowds? Through the vile atmosphere,
    Deafening roars and dizzying rumblings stream
        Without rest. What exuberant noises sway
Around, whose raucous babel grates the ear—
    Loud, commingling voices teem from
        All parts to the harsh din the vehicles rear.

Harrowing heat suffuses the close air,
    Flush with no fragrant freshness, such as trills
From the cool countryside's ambrosial fare,
        Which can replenish with ethereal joy
    The weary heart; but dust profusely rills
        Through all its crevices—floating from where
It nestles on the roads till brushed; can buoy
    Aught worse the element? And smoke too fills
        It, rendering it unhealthy to employ.

Behold the numerous people—how they flash
    Swiftly along with an impatient pace,
Wrapped in their multifarious cares. They clash
        And jostle ceaselessly—depicted plain
    To view unresting worries on the face—
        Dulcet serenity exchanged for trash!
Feverish as wild billows in the main,
    And numberless as restless ants, they chase—
        These maniacs—their imperious love of gain.

Row after row of shops unroll to view,
    Replete with various kinds of gauds and toys—
A measureless array—sure to imbue
        The vulgar mind with wonder—truly deep!
    Though such insensate baubles—useless joys!
        The works of vanity in all their new
Splendour display their emptiness—to reap
    A harvest of these luxuries employs
        Man all his energies—he toils to heap.

The unquenchable desire for riches wreathes
    Its adamantine tendrils round their souls.
Of their characteristics fully breathes
        This, the sincerest element: supreme
      Inspirer, gloriously it shines and rolls
        Their loftiest star. This fatuous yearning seethes
Within them like a flame. They fervently deem
    True wisdom lies in those, on whose lives' scrolls
        Success imprints the words—these with wealth gleam.

Hoping to reach this glittering jewel they
    Worship and idolize incessant toil,
Beneath whose vulgar and detestable sway
        Pettiness chains their wretched spirits. Ill
    Must be the vast, laborious mass—whose soil
        Manured with avarice can aught display
But noxious plants? They go on plodding till
    They wrap about their minds an ample coil
        Of cares—cares most of which their own selves will.

Their joys and griefs not on themselves depend
    But on their riches: having these—enwreathes
Happiness their ignoble minds; but rend
        Such props away, and they will swiftly sink
    In hopeless misery. This shows worth breathes
        Not in themselves, but their possessions lend
Them a reflected glory. Never think
    From trash one can steal peace, which only sheathes
        Its splendour in the minds, which from nought shrink.

They revel in the inanity of noise;
    Vociferous tumult wildly rings and strays
Through the dark tunnel of their lives; their joys
        Are loud, and sordid strife crashes and reels
    Through the resounding arches of their days;
        They founder in the stormy sea of toys—
So veritably worthless; their course wheels
    From youth to dotage through a waking maze
        Of dreams, which print their minds with their vile seals.

They notice human works alone and heed
    Only the social scene; no mysteries
Throb through the spacious universe, which need
        Wonder and awe; wrapped in sweet hopes—how strong!—
    Of prosperous days without an end quite cease
        For them great Nature's splendours—clouds may speed
With rhythmical serenity along;
    The stars may shimmer blithely; golden bees
        May hum—or all her glories form one song.

But peace! Though frivolous minds may weave a state
    Of base corruption, fluttering poisonous leaves,
Which not a single thought can decorate,
        Noble or beautiful in any way;
    Though their rank sense of happiness receives
        Never a tinge of aught sublime or great,
Like those inspiring stars—enough! Though they
    Are hateful, blissful perfect peace now heaves
        Its freshening breath—may this in my heart stay!

Despair

When hopes that roused the heart are laid asleep,
 Bequeathing wan despair alone to rear
 Its withered leaves, then dolorous tumults tear
The spirit, ruining it with lightning sweep;
Just as the pulsing ripples of the deep,
 Floating low, slumberous chimes to the pleased ear,
 Are blown by whirlwinds in their fleet career
Into wild surges, from which fierce peals leap;
I can feel nothing flowing in the stream
 Of time, which flushes me with sunlit joy;
 But I see only labyrinths, which teem
With empty things, serving but to destroy
The mind with weariness; I cannot dream
 That life is anything but a trifling toy.

To the Moon

From your gentle and elfish face,
    Cold, delicate light
    Throws rills of white,
Ethereal beams, which grace
    The peace of the night.

With tenderest smiles you soothe
    The blue of the sky,
    On whose breast you lie
Like the spirit of peace—so smooth
    You look to the eye.

Aerial beauty enwreathes
    Your enchanting flame.
    From your shimmering frame
A subtle elegance breathes
    That is hard to name.

Along the heavens aloft—
    Never astray
    From your gentle way—
You glide, with motion as soft
    As the flight of day.

Peacefully play some clouds,
    Which your beams make bright.
    Now your fairy light—
Concealed by their folds—enshrouds
    Itself from the sight.

And now you display again
　　Your countenance,
　　And you sweetly glance
On the parting clouds and rain
　　Soft rays on their dance.

The night is ineffably calm.
　　Not a cricket sings,
　　But over all things
A silence as soothing as balm
　　Unfolds its wings.

Like breaths of the balmy night,
　　Cool breezes blow
　　And freely throw
Fresh fragrance wherever their flight
　　Leads them to go.

The grass on which I recline
　　To watch your serene
　　Career, is green
And dewy, and you entwine
　　It with silvery sheen.

The gentle and sinuous stream,
　　Which flows by this place,
　　Has caught your face
In its mirror, where you beam
　　With a wavering grace.

Such enchanting delight you show
　　As you onward sweep
　　That the stars dare not peep
From their chinks, for shame that they glow
　　So feebly. They sleep.

Oh, fairest of Nature's fays;
　　When you blithely shine,
　　More rapture is mine
Than from anything fancy displays—
　　However divine.

How good to be here alone.
　　Solitude's rain
　　Touching the plain
Of the heart, soft peace is sown
　　And blossoms again.

Your influence gives fresh balm
　　To my feverish soul.
　　When I see you roll,
How deeply engraved is calm
　　On my spirit's scroll!

Rapture

A gleam of deep delight, which softly flings
    Itself at times upon the yearning soul,
    Can so transform it that it seems to roll
Through a fine dream, borne on ambrosial wings;
But ah! Such rapture as this only sings
    A moment, and the leaf of joy we stole
    A while since from the disappointing scroll
Of life is being torn to shreds and strings;
The lulling tones of the cool, gentle breeze,
The murmurings of peaceful, golden seas,
    The bubbling music of the winding stream,
The songs of swarms of honey-gathering bees—
    All these sweet things upon us only beam
    An instant, soon to flow off like a dream.

The Roll of Time

In time's eternal stream,
    All things must wave and move,
Ramble awhile and beam.
Then—flimsy ruins—shrink,
    Never to rise above
Again but feebly sink.

Its course is swift and soft,
    Wafting the universe,
Which floats and flames aloft.
Its subtle spells arrange—
    Now form and now disperse—
All works with thrilling change.

How did it first begin?
    If there was birth at all,
Will never reel within
Our knowledge. That may be
    Its end—can that befall?—
Is a deep mystery.

With fiery force it sweeps
    Sublimely on and on,
And nothing ever keeps
Its flow a moment back,
    But days are come and gone
Ere we can trace its track.

Blithely my spirit sings
    In praise of marvellous time
Because it changes things;
For if the same these stay,
    Monotonous would the chime
Of life be day to day.

Then, mighty time! Oh hail!
    Welcome the destined course,
Which you have still to sail;
What blossomy joys are strown
    Along your banks your force
Has now and then upthrown!

The Floating Cloud

Careering far away near heaven's brim
    Floats the white piece of cloud with shimmering speed,
    And now up the blue sky it must proceed,
According to the light wind's fanning whim.
How gay it looks in its soft, fleecy trim
    While waving gently like a tremulous reed!
    In the beholder what joy it can breed!
How sweet it is to see it shine and swim!
As it pursues its sinuous course there stray
    From its irregular aides light shards, which fly
For a short while and then dissolve away;
At last its radiant flight comes to a stay,
    When the colossal cloud, which clothes the sky,
    Absorbs it as it blithely passes by.

On a Bridge

Crowds jostle and struggle with importunate haste,
    From busy shops and offices set free;
Bicycles roll and rickshaws creak as fast
As weary legs could run; cars rumble past,
    Honking in impatient majesty.

Ripply with the tender touch of the breeze,
    To the parting sun a murmur of song of love,
The river glides along at sinuous ease;
Below, a gentle dream of perfect peace:
    A discordant scene of raucous tumult above!

THE FLOWERY COUNTRY

COUNTRY

WITH INTRODUCTORY NOTE ON AMORPHOUS VERSE

Introductory Note on Amorphous Verse

Poetry was originally conceived of as being absolutely distinct from prose in form and content. As regards form, verse is characterized by metre and rhyme and is divided into lines; its language is out of the ordinary and tends to picturesqueness. Wordsworth started to break down the distinction in language between poetry and prose by eliminating a superabundance of poetic expressions.

Later, there developed free verse in which the peculiar form of verse was destroyed. Rhyme was rejected and metre was replaced by a freer rhythm. However, the division into lines was retained—apparently to preserve a semblance of poetic form. In free verse, a passage is arbitrarily divided into lines of longer or shorter length according to the fancy of the writer.

If we proceed a step further and abolish division into lines, there will be no formal distinction between verse and prose. This type of verse may be termed *amorphous verse*. It has no regular shape; in form it looks like prose. There is no regular metre or regular rhyme.

However, if it is to be verse, it must differ from prose in language; it must retain what is commonly termed *poetic language*. Amorphous verse should cultivate picturesqueness, making liberal use of metaphors. Its sentences may be structurally distorted and may not resemble ordinary prose. It should possess a rhythm not too unlike the rhythm of verse; alliteration and rhyme may be freely scattered.

Its content must be treated with a poetic touch. Poetry is the expression of emotion in unusual language. To be poetry, this type of composition must be imbued with emotion—it must not be cold or dispassionate. It must be a statement of personal reaction to phenomena—an emotional reaction. The aim is not scientific truth but aesthetic pleasure. Any subject may be dealt with, provided the treatment bears the imprint of the poetic spirit.

We thus see that in point of form, amorphous verse does not differ from prose, but as regards language and content, it is distinctive. It is as much verse as free verse. It is but the logical outcome of the breakdown in the form of verse; it is only carrying free verse one step further. However, poetry is not principally a matter of metre and rhyme and distinct lines; these are merely aids to the expression of poetic values. Without them, a composition may still be poetry. What makes a poet is his mind, not language, though to be regarded as such he has to clothe his thoughts and feelings in appropriate language.

The Flowery Country

— 1 —

A tick in time is five millennia and a speck in space is the rotating, revolving spheroid: strange that change unfolded in one country a variegated series of enthralling pageants, smoothly bound like links in a chain; a land against which swings the vast Pacific, flushed by summer and crushed by winter. Cling to its fertile floor hundreds of millions, smiling, weeping, chattering, fighting, marrying, breeding, perishing. Ah! No history trails such length, flowing without surcease, like a sinuous river, now translucent, now turbid: eunuchs and beauties, soldiers and emperors, artists and thinkers, love and rancour, war and peace. The tale is limned in torpid tomes; prick and fetch the meaning who can: array the oysters of events—display from them the pearls of sense!

— 2 —

The nebulous herald of history is sweet legend. What an admirable adze had Pan Ku, and what an arduous arm! Creator of the heavens and earth, behold him stand, shaping the cosmos out of primeval chaos! Rose the masculine sun and the feminine moon; shimmered the stars; spread the terrestrial world. This first man panted and passed away like any mortal; even in death he was beneficent; metamorphosed his head to heavy hills and blood to whirling waters and breath to wandering winds. A god in his work, yet not eternal life was his; majestic Zeus, on Mount Olympus nodding and serenely surveying with a sneer the human scene, performed less, but honour floated towards him and pleasure wreathed him round. Pleasure, avaunt! Let us have toil! Till with a will life's fruitful soil!

— 3 —

Rolled aeons, and the first rulers of the Black-Haired People rose. Fu Hsi constructed houses and founded marriage, and a comfortable community, an oasis in the desert of barbarism, took form and flourished by the banks of the Hwang Ho. The basis of society then as now is agriculture: Shen Nung beheld the loess, sowed and reaped, and cereals came to grace the frugal repasts. The nation scaled, and the Hundred Families were welded into one by Huang-Ti; by land and water traffic travelled; creaked the carts and wriggled the boats. The founders of civilization: honour be to the ancients for their conception of such figures! Romulus, after embroiling his hands in fratricide, erected Rome; Norse fancy reeled and revelled in Odin and Valhalla. Away, away with horror and homicide; dream of romantic peace with the palms that abide!

— *4* —

Yao surveyed his rustic realm with reflective mien and saw the farmers and fishermen painting their days with bliss and chanting blithely at their work, and he smiled and smelled the rose of reward. His life was simple, altruism his creed. He swam for a successor not among his kinsmen, and a peasant assumed the burden. Filial piety was Shun's of magnanimous magnitude; his ferocious family with flame and flint sought to enclose him in death's cave: he still remained their selfless slave. Justly and gently did he reign, and blessings from all mouths blew toward him like softest zephyrs. The Golden Age—did fact fit in with fame? What matters? It enshrined an inspiring ideal—ideal of genuine service to the masses, not the claptrap of pliant politicians, vile, vociferous, nor the thunder of Caesarism, sans sense, sans soul.

— *5* —

A babe was piping its entry into the world: Yu heard his son's shrill voice and paused, not to pass his threshold, for he was heaving with a herculean task, the taming of China's Sorrow, that treacherous river, which mocks at human ants and ever and anon unleashes its submerging fury. After tedious years, prosperity returned and the verdant fields waved their grain-bearing stalks in lucid triumph. The engineer became the Son of Heaven. A ruler should scrupulously scrutinize his domains with his own eyes, and the Great Yu roamed far and wide in chariots and in boats. His feudal governors could not but be loyal and made their obeisance with alacrity, zealous to serve the benign "One Man."

— *6* —

Justice in high or low is the gem of conduct; in a prince it is his paramount pearl. Personal access was easy, and the four instruments of rattle, triangle, drum, and gong were ready to usher the humblest subject into the presence of his sovereign for a tale of woe or a word of advice. Tears mantled his mien at the sight of malefactors. Their misdeeds from his imperfect government drifted. Conquer not by force: the chieftain of the Miao allegiance swore, by superior goodness vanquished. Might is oft wrong: right is oft might.

— 7 —

From Yu forth flowed the initial dynasty, the Hsia; no such plan was his, but the people chose his son, upright and worthy of his father. Thus, many a line derives its depraved career: one noble person breeds a spawn of pests—of fools, the frantic, and fiends. Benevolent despotism is antiquated. Wrong it would not be if a series of Socratic sages could be ensured, but alas for Confucius and Plato and their mouldy reveries! The story of the Middle Kingdom is a string of families, each dating from a shining meteor only to terminate in a morass of chaos and cries; yet the populace ever hung their hopes on the superman.

— 8 —

Centuries sauntered by with epicurean occupants of palaces, who loafed and drank and dissipated and killed with careless callousness. The peasantry followed their furrows, their horizon circumscribed. They toiled from dawn to dusk, perpetuated their race, made sacrifices to their ancestors, and worshipped Heaven; serenely sailed their years, their one worry taxes. Thus it was; thus it has been! Came a fierce tyrant, who, like all such, was whipped by the whims of a worse woman. As confident in his permanence on his throne as that the sun would always shine in the cerulean vault, he squandered and slew recklessly. Tang was incited to unroll his banner, and the reprobate Chieh was demolished.

— 9 —

Began the Shang Dynasty, and the inexorable cycle repeated itself. Tang reigned a model monarch. Smile at the story of the removal of the bitter drought when the crops withered and famine filled its mouth. Had his corruption angered Shang Ti? he asked in all sincerity as he prayed in his holy grove of mulberries. No! Came straight and swift the response, for tumbled a refreshing shower of rain out of the cloudless sky: hearts thrilled and throbbed and lips praised him who was beloved of the Power Divine.

— 10 —

Pause and ponder: this period is more than three thousand years ago ere Homer sang the legend of doomed Troy and the fleet-footed Achilles and the wily Ulysses, when Europe seethed a wilderness, reverberating with lupine howls and ursine growls. Hard it is to dissever fact from fiction, but it is immaterial for these pages; suffice it that a civilization unfurled its foliage, and, for centuries to come, the environing tribes continued to wrap themselves in the stout, abysmal cloak of barbarism, unable to create or imitate. Without deep impulse from outside, by force of genius and originality, the gifted race expanded and blossomed. Rome was a luminous empire, yet awhile and she fell to the Germanic hordes, though war was her nectar: her loathing legacy entwined her ruin. The principal threads of the web woven in that remote antiquity stood undamaged: Huns could not unravel nor time crumble.

— *11* —

A fantastic facsimile of him who was displaced by his distinguished ancestor reappeared in Chou Hsin; a man of stupendous strength, able to bend tough iron bars, his pleasures were numberless and neurotic. What preserved his physique? Bloomed gardens in winter with artificial flowers; bubbled a lake with wine where drunken guests submerged in riotous death. Caligula and Nero were in cruelty inferior; men were made to topple off a narrow, slippery rod into a furious flame below. The son of a philosophic duke arose and smote the tyrant.

— *12* —

The longest dynasty, the Chou, which dragged a nerveless existence of more than eight hundred years, was contemporaneous with the history of famed Hellas from its dimmest dawn to its final fall. King Wu, though of martial prowess, was unenamoured of strife; like all right rulers, anxious happiness to promote and life to preserve. The six Boards were set in motion; historians records wrote, and scholars were reverenced. The humblest wearer of straw sandals could rise from penury to power. Brothers and uncles in royal palaces usually don the smile of treachery—the Duke of Chou was a rare phenomenon, a phoenix among the birds, a unicorn among the quadrupeds.

— *13* —

The boil of feudalism ripened to purulence; as successive sovereigns slept, the many states, great and small, thrived in vicious strength, and disintegration cantered briskly. Intrigue was an ardent art and shifting boundaries the trade in statecraft's mart. Alas, that factious strife is innate to man! The princes of medieval Europe pranced and slew in a maelstrom of mischief. Feudalism, your name is Chaos! A paltry baron was a prod of destiny; were millions of fine, healthy hearts meant for the playthings of a score of the vilest brains? Let the unit be humanity; it ever remains. Where are the passionate potentates? heaves the hurricane and howls.

— 14 —

The Royal Territory shrank in size and stood where the Yellow River starts to stare straight eastward to the sea, engirdled on all sides by more powerful, independent provinces: the Son of Heaven was a vassal to his vassals. War, unwearied war, did the dukes fight to annihilate one another, caring naught for the people; into oblivion dozens of states screamed. Neighed horses and clashed chariots; dwells romance in it? Incarnate sordidness! In the wild west, Chin, hardened by contact with the Tartars, held the lead. Faithlessness and ferocity marked its line of chieftains: militarism the morbid music rang. The titular sovereign, old and feeble, was hurled aside: one by one crashed the realms. Shut the Period of the Warring States: opened a new era.

— 15 —

Wheel from this desolate arena of hate; oh wheel to the more solid shelters of sense! The representatives of the king of Cochin-China were directed homeward by a compass, a magnetic hand revealing the south. Developed craftsmanship. How beautiful is jade! Green, lucent, smooth, strong, cool to the touch, capable of emitting a dulcet sound. Decorations and bowls were exquisitely carved with surpassing skill; not a few were the materials utilized—silk and leather, copper and gold; commemorative tripods of bronze were cast. Artistic beauty was well beloved—music and pictures and statues and houses.

— 16 —

Thought forms of human attributes the peak: the jewel, truth, is difficult to seek. Even if the beliefs were false, the quest, the exercise of mind, is itself a good. Curiosity is not a fault; it gives life salt. Over the sea of unrest, serenely flew a variety of philosophers, each attempting to prove the genuine way of life. Not true are their systems; the reflective can sift the wheat from the chaff. They concentrated chiefly on politics and morals, to them synonymous, their aim the happiness of humanity, the furtherance of fraternity, the promotion of peace. Unlike the Greeks, whose musings were theoretical, abstract, imbued with the pursuit of knowledge for its own sake, they were practical, responding to the diurnal demands of the common man: their teachings savour of the balm of religion. They faithfully practised what they fervently preached: sages of modern ages write with their brains, not their hearts, discourse with their tongues, not with deeds. Hence philosophy has dived into the quagmire of disrepute in the West as a mass of technicalities and distinctions, and systems come and go, like a series of dark, fragmentary dreams.

— 17 —

Laotze beheld the world in hazy light; his universe was arrayed in mysterious calm. Freedom he craved and work-a-day values he disdained. Tao, ineffable, infinite, eternal, the Law Supreme, breathing through every entity its harmony—it spells the loftiest glory. Self-cultivation in solitude stands the highest moral rule. Withdraw from the world; contemn its futile conventions and its mischievous, arbitrary laws; be one with nature; reach to perfect peace and absolute abandonment of will; let the Tao wrap you in its mystic fold: a wondrous person will emerge. You shall fly through the clouds like a bird or walk through the solid hills; you shall not dissolve and die; you shall live like a fairy for aye. Not without reason did Taoism degenerate into the handmaiden of magic, though it was noble—of metaphysical theories the profoundest ever produced beneath the earth-enclosing sky.

— 18 —

Confucius came with his golden mean: filial piety is the foundation of virtue; make the Five Relationships sweetly bloom; enjoy in moderation with honest wealth; behave in accordance with your fated position; be a diligent scholar and a just official. Verily curious that the ordinary gentleman should shine the ideal! The emperor is the Son of Heaven; he rules by right divine. An example of wisdom and virtue, his people will follow as grass bends under the winds; a monarch not living up to the fossilized code might be dethroned: result perennial insurrections, for ambition has a good excuse. No conception the sage of religion revolved of the mystery of the universe. Tradition! Tradition! New ideas were obnoxious. How did his system come to captivate fancy, to inspire veneration? Inertia is as strong as granite, easier changeless to remain. Practical value it had, for with its coherence and stress on justice, it served as a beacon to palliate ills; the Roman Empire might have lasted long and its gods of the world conferred more happiness if it possessed such a workable theory of benevolence.

— 19 —

Simplicity and frugality, preached Mo Ti. Why wear expensive silk? Why hearken to idle music? Great Yu abode in thrift and the people reposed in bliss. Self-abnegation, amounting to saintliness—unto what end? Mundane prosperity! Holiness with a utilitarian aim—could man continue long to practise this? He lost in the struggle for ideological sway. Universal, impartial, and illimitable love; a rare few might imbibe this beaming tonic, not the ruck of flesh and blood. Heaven and hell and an anthropomorphic deity—Mohism failed while Christianity flourished. Morbid moralities move not: the expectation of an imminent establishment of the Kingdom of God on earth formed the mirage among a downtrodden multitude, enmeshed in monstrous penury.

— 20 —

Not the thinkers but a warrior unity gave to the troubled land: not eloquence and righteousness but the sword and the burning brand. The First Chin Emperor overwhelmed his rivals and forged peace—the peace of terror. His sole aim was the permanence of his dynasty, ignoble and doomed to ironic failure. Good oft emerges strangely from evil, and in the process he achieved what nobody else could: China might have petrified into an array of perennially sovereign nations with resultant, ever-recurring wars and possibly the extinction of her culture. Iron will raised the Great Wall, and the Huns trekked in search of other pastures, divided the empire into thirty-six provinces with a civil service, and feudalism toppled to the dust, made into flame the books of pedants with unfortunately no stimulus to fresh creation. With no sublime objective nor goodness, yet productive of a rare effect, let his name not be held in hatred but respectful tolerance. Should not the age through its cauldron of chaos burst? He was only of his contemporaries the first.

— 21 —

The permanent curse of autocracy is impermanent utility. Terror as an instrument pants but a short span; leagued with ability it awes but with feebleness inspires contempt. The Second Emperor seized the throne through deception, forcing the heir to suicide; he sawed in two his father's clever, albeit unscrupulous, minister, and was killed by an evil eunuch who wielded the real power. Under the next ruler rebellion was triumphant; thus departed the ambitious dream of the conqueror—he sowed and others reaped.

22

A village superintendent was leading criminals to erect a monstrous mausoleum; some escaped and to save his neck he made himself the leader of the rest. Joining a powerful rebel, he somersaulted into prominence; capturing the capital, he hauled the hearts of the populace with his considerate character; defeating his rivals, he emerged an emperor. The right man to obliterate the rancour of compulsory unification glittered Liu Pang, shrewd, responding to the role he should play. He could forgive and inspire veneration: safety beaconed the universal yearning, and he made it his tenacious task. His humble origin was his educator in soaring eaglelike out of the din.

23

When Augustus was shedding his effulgent light in Rome, a boy reigned over the Celestial Empire; his minister killed him with a poisoned cup of wine at the winter solstice. The ruthless usurper, Wang Mang, conceived iconoclastic ideas of socialist hue: he enforced land nationalization, price control, taxation of incomes, and manumission of slaves. Outstanding was his originality, a trait loathed in most ages. He knew recurring rebellions; the "Red Eyebrows" roamed the country. Seized, his hated head was smashed by the mob in furious sport. A genuine revolutionary, he perished in disgrace and bequeathed his name a byword of villainy. His methods were none of the best; he nestled in cruelty's nest; more rabid rulers without ideals posterity did not so wildly detest: the cause his courage in casting convention.

24

From this blossomy dynasty the traditional China, culture definite, firmly forged, commences its career: its hallowed name remains the racial designation. Expanded the territory, notably under Wu Ti, to the tremendous, unified area ringing through the vault of time, elsewhere unknown. Through deserts and mountains journeyed Chang Chien and Li Kuang-li to Bokhara and Ferghana, and the distant countries of Central Asia leaped into the knowledge of the court and briskly trotted the caravan of trade. Glided into a dream a man of gold—reference to the Buddha, Ming Ti was told—a foreign creed its influence now unrolled. Ideal Taoism was incited and intoxicated into a superstitious religion; dull Confucianism was exalted and enthroned the official norm, and the Five Classics were inscribed on stone. Critical history was composed by Sau-ma Chien and his successors. The epochal invention of paper was like the collapse of a horrible dam in the river of learning.

— 25 —

Han fell and a dark, deep spell of disintegration swept. The struggle for power tore the empire into shreds that coalesced for a while to form three states. Hovers affectionate romance round the three comrades of the Peach-Orchard Oath, unbreakably sealed in blood. A penurious maker of straw sandals, Liu Pei became the emperor of the mountainous west. Love and hate with the ancients was strong; in a story must prance a villain to make it boil, and Tsao Tsao, the founder of the northern state of Wei, fulfils the invidious role. Self-sacrifice, heroism, guile, treachery, bloodshed yelled in the meaningless ocean of conflict; ceased in due course the Three Kingdoms under the rule of the most depraved of dynasties, the Tsin.

— 26 —

Unity was ephemeral as a dream: rolled in the Huns and chaos reigned supreme. North flew from south; diverse barbarian lines fought furiously through half the land while the other saw the rise and fall of a succession of incapable despots. The country wore an abject aspect of doom—even exuberant optimists might quiver with inquietude at its future—yet it merged engirdled in luminous light and splendid might: draw the clear moral who will. Four centuries of turmoil—how could flesh and blood endure? Misery, misery! Myriads shrieked into dark death. An emperor wept a slave; a waif smiled ruler; one sovereign raved a lunatic; another gleamed a pious vegetarian. Blended Chinese and Tartars, and the latter lost their identity. Alien rulers must eventually evaporate if few they remain and cannot engulf the original populace: the race that inhabits owns the land.

— 27 —

But the stream of progress flowed resistless; armies tore throats with madness dancing in their eyes while the people worked with patience in their hearts. For the first time swayed Tartars the Middle Empire, and by its adoption showed how invulnerable stood the rock of her civilization; captive Greece a smaller triumphal arch over her conquerors raised. Apt pupils were they: shone bright the Toba. Soared sculpture: colossal statues were carved in caves. The first pagodas reared their storeys to publish spiritual flight. Often a less pretentious product spells a greater good: bubbled a humble beverage, tea, and engendered sobriety.

— 28 —

Confusion advances and retreats: ebbed the dark tide of passionate pain. Tang smiled and culture shimmered in full bloom. The actual founder, Li Shih-min, the greatest monarch to don the yellow robe, reclined his rule on popular praise. Wisely he remarked: as a boat floats on water that can overturn it, so a sovereign leans on the people who can withdraw their support. Not consumed by ardour of conquest, he conquered; other nations he could understand and over Asia flowed his fame. Learning he loved; clever, courageous, gracious, he was the paragon of the world of his time. Ambassadors and merchants assembled in the capital. When foreigners came without malevolent mien and wily webs of conquest, welcome beamed: only in later ages dawned the desire to dwell alone. All religions raised their shrines in Changan; not only the Three Creeds, but Nestorianism, condemned in the West, Zoroastrianism, fleeing from Persia, Islam, militant elsewhere but peaceful in contact with light. Let his luminous effluence never be dim. Few are the rulers who practise this truth. Power is service.

— 29 —

The curse of an absolute monarch is the ease with which he falls to a favourite; the tyrants ever bowed disastrously to the Yin principle. Wu Tse-tien strangled her baby, tortured the empress, poisoned her husband, and reigned a masculine emperor. Cruel, licentious, she dominated for half a century, giving the nation a profile of prosperity. She is loathed by her country's historians while her counterpart, Catherine of Russia, is hailed "the Great." To the East virtue, to the West glory! Sat Ming Huang on the throne; a bonfire he heaped of silks and jewels. The Han Lin Academy he founded; conquests he made; his pear garden heard poets recite and actors chant. Died he at fifty, and his memory would have wafted fragrance down the avenue of the ages. Old, he fell beneath the dissolute sway of Yang Kuei-fei, revelled and ruined. Revolution and disgrace: how many rulers thus crashed? Romance or folly? Anyway, the people paid.

— 30 —

A dynamic dynasty of culture and power; the country thrived in spite of civil war and many vacuous emperors. Did not rulers die from quaffing elixirs of immortality? Did not eunuchs triumph? Fruitful intercourse with foreign nations; influence glorious; came Japan, Korea, Annam to imbibe and imitate the civilization. Not by force of arms were they compelled to learn: they flocked from admiration. What body of poetry surpasses the Tang? Half a hundred thousand poems survive its genius to attest; romantic Li Po warbled of wine and nestled in nature. Painting soared to the pitch of perfection: Wu Tao-tzu and his landscapes of peerless power. Printing, than which a more beneficial invention never saw the light, effected its happy entry: books, most precious of possessions, to all available grew.

— *31* —

A drunken emperor was imprisoned by his eunuchs; a brutal general had them slain, then murdered him and performed the trick of placing a boy on the throne for two years ere formally taking the empire himself. In danced confusion: five short dynasties hovered over a space of as many decades. Turkomans enacted a colossal role in the sordid drama, and Kitais rushed raids from the North, slaughtering with stupendous zest. Why surged no democratic or socialist movements? Why wearily sighed the masses inert? Not true that plight must spawn wild revolution; no spirited genius dreamed a new solution.

— *32* —

An army was tramping to crush invaders; roused was the general from a sodden stupor in his tent and wrapped in the flowing imperial robe to the vociferous clangour of acclaim. The sovereign, a child, was lifted from his throne through no fault of his family. Perilous was the nexus between a boy and a station of onerous duties, averred the conspiring officers; had this shone their genuine thought, the bird of hereditary monarchy should have flown: no such conclusion did they reach. From Chao Kuang-yin the Sung Dynasty of three centuries flowed; a case was ever ready to prance in favour of a usurper with this luck. All the harbingers of lengthy lines were good; did not virtue wreathe their hearts, or how could their scions hold a mandate from heaven so prolonged? What light of logic could more strongly gleam? Gods and men love the favourites of fortune. Rebel who fails a traitor is: who wins receives a hero's bliss!

— 33 —

Inglorious fretted the dynasty militarily. The Liaos maintained their depredations and levied oppressive subsidies; uprose their vassals, the Chin, who entombed their power to the melody of a rippling river and drove the Sung to the Yangtze, where for half its duration it fluttered helpless pinions. See the keen, patriotic sword of Yo Fei flash and drop; to the last loyal in defence of his country, he was dragged to prison for treason—his accuser, a collaborator, a minister enmeshed in the lime of avarice, won the worthless emperor's ear—and perished a felon's fate. The crime of a martyr is virtue.

— 34 —

Philosophy, poetry, and painting suspended radiant blossoms: scholarship soared. An idealist, an original economist devoted to the cure of poverty and the promotion of public welfare, Wang An-shih unfurled a social experiment whose leaves in the fierce light of practice wilted. Ships sailed in trade to foreign lands; trotted the crafts apace; went hand in hand utility and beauty. Who says Cathay fell into dreamless slumber from an early cycle? The planet of sweet progress ever was in motion. Hangchow a spell flung over Marco Polo with its splendour and arresting wealth: twelve thousand bridges of stone, numberless mansions, inhabitants apparelled in silk, vast volumes of trade; its beauty is embodied in a proverb.

— 35 —

Greatest of conquerors, Genghis Khan, dark terror of the earth: in youth he steeped his foes to boil in cauldrons. Grand Khan of the savage Mongols, he emerged from his desert capital of Karakoram to pile mountains of skulls and level shining cities to the dust; he swept over the China of the Golden Horde and all Asia, this destructive tempest. Kublai, his grandson, attacked the Sungs, the last of whom, an infant, sank on the back of his commander beneath the bubbling sea, where floated a hundred thousand corpses. Planted for the first time a barbarian a genuine dynasty over the whole of the Celestial Empire. What shall we say of him, this man, who was overlord of Asia and Eastern Europe? With ruthless ambition fraught, yet reigned he a good ruler, better than any Tartar and many a man of civilized ancestry. Peking he built for his capital, so superb succeeding dynasties inherited it.

— 36 —

Faded the leaf of the Yuan with fleetest ease, corroded by the canker of futile luxury and fuming corruption; long did the barbarians fight to forge their sway and they fulfilled the stern, periodical task of reunification—alas!—so oft performed, so oft undone. No fragrant flower of innovation did they bring, though swift to absorb they hurt not learning. The Germanic hordes reduced to rubble the Roman Empire: glowered in wildness the Dark Ages. Not so with the Tartars trampling across the Yellow River. Proves not this the difference of stability of the two cultures?

— 37 —

Heavy taxation and evil government fanned the natural hatred of foreign emperors: rebels flourished like grass. Chu Yuan-chang, who had lost the whole of his family in a devastating plague and served in a monastery, enlisted in an insurgent band and created a commanding name. With wisdom imbued, he won the adherence of other groups and obtained their aid; ascending the ladder of success, he drew admiration, the focus of popular pride. A comet streamed the ominous herald of the downfall of the obnoxious dynasty: the Mongol sovereign leaped like a hare into the wilderness.

— 38 —

Gleams the Ming Dynasty with a peculiar glory—the child of patriotism. The illiterate progenitor, designated Hung-wu, ruled mildly; he simplified the legal system and promoted education. Resuscitating ancient practices, naught he did original—a model monarch; he fought as much as needful to maintain his realm. A benevolent despot, he could be cruel when his power was in peril and died bequeathing an odorous memory and his body reposed in a magnificent mausoleum in Nanking.

— 39 —

Ascended the throne with tremulous steps his grandson, a boy; soon overthrown in anguished war, into obscurity and peace he dived in the robe of a monk. Dark cruelty to power may issue in capable rule: Yung Lo, who scattered massacre through all his opponents, acted in this wise. He reconstructed Peking, subdued Mongolia and Tongking, and put two thousand scholars to the compilation of a gigantic encyclopaedia. Cruised a fleet of junks along the coasts of southern Asia to receive mild homage—touching at Cambodia, Siam, Borneo, Java, Sumatra, Malacca, Burma, Bengal, Ceylon, and Aden.

— 40 —

Arrived the line's allotted span: toppled the empire into a whirlpool of clangourous din. Brushed by the rays of meritless victory, stood Li the rebel by Peking's stout walls, beheld gates slide apart by treachery, and sat in triumph in the palace halls. In a San Kuan temple, the emperor fatuously beseeched of the gods—escape or suicide; receiving the response he climbed up Prospect Hill, inscribed with his blood a moving message and dangled himself on a tree. The wanton usurper seized the favourite beauty of Wu San-kuei, who in his amorous ire retraced his steps to Shan-hai-kuan and offer made to the willing Manchus to ride through the Great Wall and render him aid. The vanquished brigand looted, fled, and perished in ignominy. For the land's loss, who was to blame—a worthless sovereign, a thoughtless general, a licentious rebel?

— 41 —

Designed from birth to rule, their work they do not comprehend: the prerogative of monarchs. Every line was a desert with few oases and the Ming formed no exception. Could a viler stench be wafted abroad than the misrule of those ludicrous deformities, eunuchs? The popular notion of family property consigned the empire to the nominal rule of children. The progress of culture almost came to a halt: scholasticism dragged its dreary chains. Philosophers, poets, artists, and craftsmen were not so great as of old; officials were pedants who chanted the classics, fancying truth within their purview, all problems soluble with their wands. Bounded in over the seas the Portuguese, imperialism their creed, rapacious greed their idol, cruelty their craft—portentous heralds of the woes to come.

— 42 —

The Manchus, a tribe of the Nuchen Tartars, originally lived vassals of the Mings. Swore Nurhachu and fished Manchuria into his net; a son he left to scheme to fact his ambitious dream. A tiny race rapped at the gates of a vast empire and rode in with ease beneath the shield of guile and treachery; slipped a distracted people into slavery's coil. Unlike most scourges of their race, these Tartars dangled dexterously the pleasing art of conciliation; Ming scions tumbled into the pit of death; the barbarians gathered the sheaf of triumph; the pigtail, novel badge of servitude, grew on all heads.

— 43 —

A second time a line of foreign Sons of Heaven, after sedulous strife, bore sway over the length and breadth of the Middle Realm. The earlier sovereigns of the Ching Dynasty—Kang Hsi, Yung Cheng, Chien Lung—governed with able hand, maintaining an enlightened government on traditional lore. Order and peace diffused their healing influence; benevolence displayed its burnish so long as power was safe—a golden sheath enclosing a bloodstained sword; population and territory increased. Weak rulers followed, havoc in their train, and the last decades of the nineteenth century witnessed the dark domination of Tzu-hsi, unscrupulous, opinionated, conservative, under whom the empire reeled like a mammoth wreck.

— 44 —

The Chinese—a lengthy history of fine glory to their credit—deemed themselves the only race of light; no wish had they to jostle and gesticulate with unwelcome strangers. Curious was their attitude though comprehensible; did not the Greeks, dispersed on islands and peninsulas, late tasters of culture, mystified by their speech and ways, as barbarous view the Persians? A people yearned to dwell aloof; what right had others to say nay, to come to its secluded shores for unpalatable intercourse and enforce their greed with cannon? Came the aggressors of a whole array of nations to carve the juicy melon.

— 45 —

The Manchus embraced conservatism from fear and ignorance; their power moulded within the framework of a mellow culture they saw change as threat to supremacy. Blind to altered conditions they hobbled helplessly toward ruin. Progress, weary in the preceding dynasty, blinked wearier eyes; smug, slumberous scholars pored as ever over stifling tomes, rifled by time of sap. Knowledge is the folly of the pedant. The profitless polity was what it had always been. The dynasty would in any case have ultimately fled—stern law of history and a legacy of Confucian monarchism—the advent of the West made its replacement assume a novel form.

— 46 —

There were who could construe the message of the day: sank Kang Yu-wei beneath the marsh of failure with a moderate system of reform to save the country; preached Sun Yat-sen a democratic republic while tyranny raved and slew and the country rocked to ruin like a tree in a violent storm. Three years ere started to stream the cannoned rhetoric of the First World War a careless bomb resounded in Wuchang; the military conspirators leaped, and the revolution took wings and rapidly flew to its goal. No long-drawn civil war ensued; the Manchus, effete, corrupt, in numbers meagre, wilted before the national blast and relinquished their sovereignty. The first republic of the East took sudden birth. If an imperial family must needs vanish, it suffers less dishonour to yield to the people than see a new house reign: its loss spells greater gain.

— 47 —

Smiled the dawn of a new era over the horizon. Would the promise reach fruition? Old ways retreat with slowest steps and the naive adoption of a foreign culture in toto by a nation drugged with ancestral worship could only engender tribulations. Ignorant would-be emperors thrived like locusts; swashbucklers overran the land, bent on enacting the drama of the bad old days. The senseless mass of contestants trampled down the waving fields of rice and wheat while foreign hawks observed with glinting eyes. Turmoil and strife, and the peasant groaned and moaned, not knowing the cause. A modicum of modernization budded in the cities. Keen was the thirst for imitation; diminutive was the power to act.

— 48 —

With mimicry indigenous in the bone, the moment peril prowled their sulphurous shores, the Japanese, in fever of ferocity, imbibed and improved. Invertebrates, they had waded through their neighbour's culture with ease and with ease revolved now toward the West and sprang a great power. Nothing original, nothing beneficial could they trickle into the mellifluous stream of progress; war was their god and China their principal goal. Manifold woes and tyrannies dispersed they with wanton hand till flesh writhed and blood boiled. Staggered a war of eight years—cities shattered, millions massacred, rage rampant—his prey the aggressor could not crush. Insane with fury, he swooped to enslave the South Seas; if the conquest of one country fled, why then, make fervent foes of all! The atomic bomb shot anguished thrills through the flatulent island empire and it shrivelled and crumbled.

— 49 —

Vanished the darkest of her dangers stalking through half a century. Was the moon of peace and prosperity to shed her radiant rays over the sorrowing soil? Myriads had to drag slow, weary steps to stricken homes for life afresh. Old penury cast its abysmal shade; industry and agriculture were primitive; famine and pestilence had always reared their gorgon heads. In filthy villages the peasants toiled from dawn to dusk, in ignorance steeped, devoid of culture, without the requisite minimum of material muscle—the muscle making existence safe and joyous. But horrors need not elude control and an earnest will to accomplishment strikes not the wall of eternal frustration. Ideals are the green-clad islands in the gloomy ocean of human woe.

— 50 —

Five thousand years appears a lengthy coil to mortal man; only one nation can unroll this tangle of time. A single culture all along pursued its sweep; progress there was but changes reached not to the deep. Billow of other values and floated an amorphous wreck. Ancient ideas continued to saunter unobtrusively through the lives of the peasantry; vociferously barked the imported doctrines. Contending parties with notions of tainted tint enthroned them panaceas. The country rang with the clash of cultures. Confucian civilization had spun its thread and limped to slumber. The Flowery Country, creating a culture from her genius, flourished in the river of time. What was to come? Our narrative at this point can cease its flow. Our theme is the glowing drama of long ago.

GRAINS OF SAND

In a Ship

The shimmering stars in profusion fill
    The vaulted face of the moonless sky,
    A nest of Daedalian clouds that fly
In amorphous gloom above the chill,
    Enveloping nights. Winds sweep and sigh:
I yearn to fathom the secrets they spill.

The rolling deep is a vast expanse
    Of mysterious motion and majesty,
    Stern in its violent energy;
Roars, issuing from the passionate dance
    Of the waste of waves, speak history
Of men and wrecks in eternal trance.

In this soothing darkness the stars invest
    My brain with serenest thoughts that bloom
    Of mild Malaya—the pleasant gloom
Of rubber plantations where squirrels jest;
    The palmy kampongs; Joy's birds assume
A brighter hue in Memory's nest.

The vessel continues its swift career;
    What a beautiful, impressive array,
    Alluring as flowers that scent and sway,
Of brilliant lights shine tier on tier:
    The romantic rock at the break of day
Will we reach. How firmly it draws near!

Shooting from the engirdling brine,
    Hong Kong, there she lies in dreamy repose!
    I can feel it breathe, can feel it close—
Its precipitous, terraced streets, which combine
    Glamour and dirt—the sunset's rose
On its peaks, the plangent bays that shine.

The Eternal Nation

Ferocious bombs let loose from the air
    On populous cities lying below.
Innocent corpses strewn on the bare
    Debris, replete with ensanguined woe.
    Horrors have been, since the world's first glow;
But could any destruction with such compare?

Fields fertile as any the earth has known
    Are relinquished while the tillers are shot;
Towns and villages are laid prone,
    And many a body is left to rot
    For the pleasure of those, whose brains are hot
With desire for the melody of man's groan.

In anguished confusion hordes leave home
    Beneath the remorseless, thundering flash.
In penurious terror the wanderers roam
    From province to province to shun the lash
    Of a rampant soldiery, who dash
To fragments Liberty's sacred dome.

From the earliest records of history,
    From the faintest twilight of her past,
Many a Hunnish calamity
    Has defiled her flourishing soil. Such vast
    Hosts of barbarians had she aghast
To face and endure sharp agony.

But though Mongol bands through the Great Wall burst,
　　Though they burned and ravaged with fiendish zeal,
The lava of misery they dispersed
　　　Was nothing compared to the streams that reel
　　　Around the land, which clearly reveal
The extent of the enemy's cannibal thirst.

Ere the glorious rise of Greece and Rome,
　　She had known for centuries time's swift flow.
Empires have glistened and vanished like foam.
　　　Her industrious people continued to grow.
　　　Could she perish? Could force overthrow
Her and create a perennial tomb?

The indignant sympathy set alight
　　In the world by the treatment she receives
From the ruthless foe: invincible right
　　　That subtly a web of power weaves.
　　　Could she fall, a bunch of filemot leaves?
Victory's sun will emerge from the night!

The Boatwoman

Down heaven's blue vault declines the sun,
　　Flinging the waves soft, farewell rays:
The weary boatwoman, her work done,
　　Sits at the stern with thoughtful gaze.

Battered and worn, bright smiles unknown,
　　Not flowers, but faded leaves her lot:
The harsh element's strength on her is shown,
　　By which her eventless life is caught.

Integral portion of the seas
　　Embodiment of innocent days:
Hers is the stoical bravery
　　Of endurance—could aught be worthier praise?

Ode to the Sea

Your waves besiege the shore,
    They throb and tremble so,
With passionate, reeling roar
That the dawn shivers, sore
    With fear of their wild flow.

Tremulously the gale
    Sweeps over your stern breast,
And, wielding its winged flail,
Makes such dire wrinkles trail
    Along your water's rest.

The fierceness of your flow
    Sheds an ineffable grace,
And, as you come and go—
A picture full of woe—
    Beauty enwraps your face.

Music is in your sound,
    Magic is in your soul:
And my whole mind is bound
To you, and all around
    I feel your influence roll.

In ceaseless motion whirled,
    Raging with harsh unrest,
With wildness round you curled,
The strife in the wide world
    Is mirrored in your breast.

How stern you are and deep:
　　Sterner than night's dark sky,
Or than the awful sweep
Of thunderstorms, which weep
　　Chill showers as they fly.

Clothed in a robe of grey
　　Clouds, waving fold on fold
Drearily dawns the day,
And the sun shoots its ray,
　　Desponding at the cold.

Dark force thrills through your waves
　　Beneath your eloquent roll;
Your passionate music paves
The air and ardently laves
　　And fills my bitter soul.

The pageant that you rear
　　So sombre and sublime,
So gloriously austere
Is that it should be dear,
　　And fixed to endless time.

Blake Pier

Crowds swirl around
In ceaseless motion;
Dainty girls trip along,
And coolies pant and shout;
Rickshaws gallop with curious ease;
Red buses pause momentarily,
Vomit, and swallow passengers,
Then lumber away with heavy tread.

I spin and face the sea:
Ships choke the spacious harbour;
Liners which cleave the ocean to Europe or America;
Coastal steamers which prowl up the Pearl River to Canton,
Or take a rocking three hours' trip to Macao;
Briskly launches scamper to and fro,
Five minutes and they hug Kowloon opposite,
Then wheeling they return.

Junks in hundreds—
Their sails of patched, brown canvas—
Lean on the ripples as they glide:
Their inmates, dull and worn,
Men, women, children,
And land an alien element—
Cheerless human fish!

Amid this scene of noise and struggle,
Solitude, like a boa constrictor,
Grasps me in its steely folds;
All this clangorous life
A vague, confusing dream appears;
I feel as in a wilderness—
But no! That would breathe greater harmony,
An indescribable rapture;
Peace shines the jewel of the heart:
Here a teak case sheathes its light!

From Li Po

Before the couch the moonlight gleams,
Frost upon the ground it seems,
Gaze I upward; then, head lowered,
Thoughts of home enfold my dreams.

The Hut

Through the attap roof trills light,
Insects crawl to left and right,
Rock its stilts when light winds scamper—
Calmly lives the anchorite!

The Typhoon

Thick fog veils the city below;
Dark rain shoots in angry flow;
The wild typhoon, in thunderous fury,
Thrills me with a rapturous glow.

The Hawker

Two big stalls by the busy street,
Steaming with noodles, shrimps, and meat;
Fills he bowls for others—though starving,
Naught is there for him to eat!

The Bride

Glows the flowery sedan chair,
Pipes and cymbals choke the air;
All radiate joy—from home departing,
Weeps the bride with tender care.

The Street Sleeper

Torrents of rain and piercing cold,
Wind with a scythe of song in its hold;
Ragged blanket and straw on the pavement:
The weary form has a sleep of gold!

The Invader

Though the plains are overrun,
Though the cities may be won,
Triumph will not gild the invasion:
Mountains foil the myrmidon!

Balm for Misery

The tranquil sound of verdant leaves—
A tune that never cloys—
Through which its way the mild breeze weaves,
As delicate is your voice.

Such balmy kindness does it hold
My misery flashes change,
When trapped within its cage of gold,
To joy profound and strange.

So tenderly your music steals
Upon my mind, where teem
Bitterest struggles, that it heals
With swiftness of a dream.

A treasure is your winsome speech,
The key of firm release
Of solace I never thought to reach,
Warm hope and happy peace.

Never Absent

Serenely in the sky she sails,
    Her lofty glory ever new,
Aloof from earth's unquiet gales:
    I see the moon and you.

The murmuring water's melody,
    Pleasant and soft, my ear shoots through,
Its tremulous surface dipped in glee:
I see a stream and you.

In delicate poise on swaying stem,
    The blushing petals, brushed with dew,
More luminous are than purest gem:
    I see a rose and you.

On a Peak

Cool is the breeze's brush
   On my brow as I blithely lean
On the railing, tasting the hush
Of creeping time and the lush
   Splendour of the scene.

Evening makes aware
   Its magic of deepest lure,
Taste I of delicate fare—
Beauty extremely rare,
   Ineffably sweet, and pure.

The sun is a crimson ball,
   Low on horizon's rim:
Ere night displays its pall,
Clouds—varitinted shoal—
   Jostle in languorous dream.

The roofs of the city below,
   Flat mass of burnished grey,
Reflect the sunset's glow;
Along the streets in slow
   Motion specks wind their way.

The sea is a shimmering sheet
   Alive with golden rays;
Ships lie in serenest state;
Some smoothly glide on the plate
   And softly fade from gaze.

Glamorous view like this,
   Rare fruit of tree of time,
Gives thrill of sublimest bliss;
Ethereal beauty it is,
   Floated from fairy clime!

Through a Truck Window

Green curved hills lean against the azure sky,
    On top erect their strength straight firs and pines;
    Villages slumber of narrow lanes and shrines
And muddy courtyards where pigs and poultry vie;
Rice-fields beneath the golden sunlight lie,
    Stalks delicately swaying in rhythmic lines;
    Men stoop and move, fulfilling fate's designs,
Heedless of world and those who make or destroy;
Though beat time's wings with violent stress of change,
    Life here maintains its weary, slow career;
    Serenely as floating dragonflies in the air,
This scene has sailed adown the centuries' range;
To break the land's dream needs a charm how strange?
    Not trucks, nor telegraph poles, nor war so sere.

Whole Night Through

Care rolled in billows the whole night through;
    No wink of sleep befell,
Like dew, to wash the senses away,
    And purify the mind's cell.

I thought of war's engulfing rage
    And millions tossed in the groan
Of death—how old the repeated tale
    Of regions lost and won!

I thought of the joy-embowered home
    In country of sunshine and mirth;
No arrow of message covers the miles
    From land of darkness and dearth.

Victory Will Be Ours

Bright culture wafted round this land
    The perfume of celestial flowers:
The world was still barbaric sand;
    Victory will be ours!

True wisdom builds, this people rose
    And reared civilization's towers:
Vandalic are their foolish foes;
    Victory will be ours!

They love the right and loathe the wrong;
    China with all her friendly Powers;
Robbers can never prosper long;
    Victory will be ours!

The United Nations' noble aim
    Is sacred freedom, and when showers
On enemy countries their might's flame;
    Victory will be ours!

The Frivolous Woman

Futile life and frivolous brain,
Tongue of malice, vicious, vain;
Wearisome theme of the foolish idle;
When will she sow true glory's grain?

In the Village of Loping, Yunnan

August—and not a trace of heat;
Air is cool to the point of cold;
A misty rain—making temperature
Fall ten degrees—just ceased to warble
Its lyric and reluctantly withdrew;
Above frowns a cheerless sky
Clad in a robe of sombre grey.

The luxuriant grass proudly proclaims its scintillating green;
The paddy stalks wave in rhythmic grace;
The golden chrysanthemum breathes in bliss,
And the broad-leaved lotus floats in benign serenity;
From leafy pines and bamboo groves
The notes of magpies begin to trill.

As I stroll along this road of mud
With heavy heart and aching head,
Gazing at the horizon's rim,
Gazing at the dark hills clad in gloom,
Gazing at the airplanes crawling from revetments,
Gazing at the village of miserable mud huts,
My mind is in a tangle
Of thoughts that taste of pain.

How fares the home that I have not seen
For years in far-off, sun-washed Malaya?
Has the locomotive of barbaric war
Rolled heavily over it, leaving ruins?
Or has it escaped unscathed,
Surviving in peace and quiet joy?

The ferocious, anachronistic enemy,
Imitator of the Golden Horde,
A short while ago was smitten low
By a nemesis dropping from the blue;
Its boast dissolved, its empire gone,
Its lurid sun is dimmed—
And may it never flame again!

Yonder lies the wretched village,
Sleeping its sleep of squalid penury;
Stolid are the peasants in their woe,
Toiling from dawn to dusk—toiling, moiling, sweating—
Returning to repose their weary limbs
On beds of straw in vermin-infested homes!
Are they to subsist for aye like this?
Or will they live to see civilized amenities,
Their village grown to a fit abode for man?

Idealism

A painter or a novelist
    None eulogize as practical
    Who daubs or tells a sorry tale;
Stolid statesmen alone enlist
    Vociferous homage though they fail!

Only the good is worth pursuit;
    On the practice of a dazzling dream
Let genuine admiration beam;
    Lavish not praise on bitter fruit;
    Bright stars of life ideals gleam!

The Bliss of Sleep

The day is fled with its sheaf of joy and care;
    The world is one expanse of dark serene;
    Now is the time for sleep with hands unseen
To close my mind in kind oblivion's lair;
Softly and gently breathes the still night air,
    The moonlight glows a wan and slumberous sheen;
    But toss I on my pillow—what has been
Or may be turns on me its baleful glare;
    Shall I get up at dawn with languid eyes?
Shall heavy weariness claim me for her own?
Ah no, good sleep, I am your willing prize;
    Do not desert me, leaving me to moan!
My mind is blank; falls peace from out the skies;
    My senses fade; Sleep reigns upon her throne.

A Gift

A gift should not be reckoned in terms of gold,
But in the warmth of regards in it enrolled.
Many happy returns of this day to you,
And with the passing years may our friendship grow!

Alumni Reunion

Here's to the halls of HKU;
    Here's to the hostels where we dwelt,
And ate, debated, laughed and played—
    What fervour of life we felt!

Here's to our scattered pals of old;
    Here's to the excursions that we made;
And here's to lectures and exams—
    Our memories never fade!

Doctors and teachers and engineers
    Are we, with spirits gathering mould—
Drop our cares and turn our eyes
    Back to those hours of gold!

L'Envoi

Welcome, thrice welcome, guest and member,
  To this our sweet reunion here!
Farewell, farewell, guest and member;
  We'll meet again next year!

Alma Mater

Blissful was the time when we
    Sped across the ocean's brine,
And, before the break of dawn,
    Saw the tiered lights of HK shine!

Hail to her, our Alma Mater!
    What enchanting days and sweet
We spent within her shady halls,
    Gathering knowledge at her feet!

When the hour of parting came,
    We cast a backward glance to where
She stood above the city's din,
    And we felt her wisest care!

We assemble here this evening
    Through the magic of her name;
Let us pass the cup around
    To revere her quenchless flame!

Sweet Ideal

When the world is full of strife
    And the skies are wrapped in deepest gloom,
I turn my thoughts to sweetest you,
    Then glimmer afresh the flowers in bloom!

When the world is full of joy
    And I revel in the hours that shine,
I dream of those more golden days,
    When you forever will be mine.

Whether the air is clear or dim,
    Whether the minutes make or mar,
I think of you, my sweet ideal,
    My sun and moon and guiding star!

A Photo

With the beauty of the flowers you bloom,
    With the radiance of the stars you gleam;
The bewitching smile that dispels all gloom
    Is caught here, an everlasting dream;
Your eyes the rays of sweetness illume;
    On your aspect hovers of wisdom the beam!

Oh, picture dear of her I love,
    I wonder at you the livelong day;
How could I my gaze remove
    From the glamorous visage you display?
With you beside me I feel my dove,
    My life, is not so far away!

Love Perennial

I'll love you whether the heavens
    Clamour with showery din
Or gleam with serenest light—
    I'll love you through thick and thin!

What tongue must fail to speak
    Or pen must fail to write:
I love you with a love
    Ineffably firm and bright!

Do you ever doubt my love?
    Do you my feelings deem
Mere vapourings of the fancy?
    Kindly not so, nor seem!

Forever will I love
    The treasure I have found;
Forever, aye forever,
    To you my heart is bound!

In a Cinema

The air-conditioned hall was cool
    In spite of the crowd within;
Sixteen to the minute flashed the pictures
    Amid bold music's din;
Struggled to their destined bliss
    The hero and heroine!

Elatedly sitting by your side
    To watch the film-spun scene;
I did not know what the figures did,
    Nor what the words might mean;
Only of you was I aware,
    Not the shadows on the screen!

As out into the air we went,
    I felt as in a trance;
The journey home I saw the stars
    Leap from their perches and dance;
Flitted all night in glamorous dream
    Your fairy countenance!

Lovely Is the Fragrant Rose

Lovely is the fragrant rose
   Amid its cluster of verdant leaves,
Washed by the falling dews of heaven,
   As gently it sways and heaves!

Lovely is the glittering goldfish
   Darting within its crystal pool,
Now singing to the moss-strewn surface,
   Now resting mild and cool!

Lovely is the circular moon
   Painting the night with silvery sheen,
Silently gliding from east to west
   With aspect softly serene!

But more lovely than all these
   Are you—oh wonder whom I adore!
Sweetest of sweets! Nonpareil!
   In the realm of beauty you soar!

Another Name

To every person cleaves a name,
    While some have more to greet;
Though little difference does it make,
    Yet a sweet name is sweet!

Fragrant is your glorious name;
    How oft do I repeat it and muse!
But I yearn to give you another name,
    Which I alone might use!

You are my lyric, the lyric I love,
    A lyric of beauty and delight!
May Lovely Lyric be your name—
    This is my copyright!

Sixty Miles Away

Sixty miles away
    Lives the love of my heart;
Sixty miles away
    We are now apart!

How I long for the hours
    Rapidly to flee,
That the sixty miles
    Might soon cease to be!

Sunday—and we should
    Be in tête-à-tête;
Oh, you sixty miles!
    Small you are and great!

Still this message shall travel
    Sixty miles away
To my Lovely Lyric—
    "I think of you all day!"

'Tis Easy

'Tis easy to fly to the stars and hear
    The music of the spheres;
'Tis easy to whirl through boundless space
    Without a tremor of fears,
       Were you beside me!

'Tis easy to scale the loftiest mountains
    In their mantles of clouds and snows;
'Tis easy to cross the rockiest passes
    Where no plant or creature grows,
       Were you beside me!

'Tis easy to make the trees to bloom
    Or fountains gush from the ground;
'Tis easy to transform the world
    And mould it flat or round,
       Were you beside me!

The Cowherd and the Weaving Girl

Long, long ago, so the legend goes,
    Met on the banks of a limpid stream
A cowherd and a weaving girl;
    And love enmeshed them in glamorous dream!

In married bliss they passed their days;
    Propitious seemed to be their fate
Until the gods in jealousy
    Cruelly made them separate.

The Milky Way—the River of Heaven—
    Was used their happiness to bar;
Apart they dwelled on either side
    Of this impassable barrier.

The Jade Emperor, slightly less unkind,
    Decreed their meeting once a year;
The gentle magpies flew a bridge
    For them together to appear!

Our love, my sweet, not less than this
    Of the Cowherd and the Weaving Girl,
Will surely endure through life, I ween,
    And happy keep as the days unfurl!

Sad, though magnificent, is their story—
    To meet but only once a year!
May we not such misfortune see,
    But be together always, dear!

How I Love You

I love you as the magnet
    Loves to turn to the north;
It never changes direction
    For all its force is worth!

I love you as the planet
    Loves to race round the sun;
It never changes its course,
    Its endless, elliptical run!

I love you as the plant
    Loves the refreshing dew;
It shines with joyous glory
    Revealed in its verdant hue!

I love you as the swallow
    Loves the clear, blue air;
Serenely it sails and dips
    Without a trace of care!

Lucky Day

The star that reigned in the sky
　　At the hour when you were born
Was the brightest that ever was,
　　The fairest that ever shone!

'Tis a lucky day to you,
　　And a lucky day to me;
Ever will it be dear,
　　Engraved in my memory!

You grew up like a flower
　　Bathed in beauty and grace;
Happy has been your life,
　　Happiness lives in your face!

This birthday is the first
　　Since into my dreams you came;
And as the years succeed
　　My love will glow the same!

Prelude

I will forever love you, dearest,
    However my lot is cast;
Always united will we be,
    Our love is meant to last!

You are the sweetest and most fair
    That ever came to birth;
You are the purest and the best,
    Unique, of flawless worth!

Sacred is this kind day of vows,
    This wondrous day of days;
Still is this hour of plighted troth
    As into your face I gaze!

I bind myself to cherish you,
    You are my all in all;
No smallest word of harsh intent
    Shall from my lips befall!

I bless this prelude to that day,
    Which time shall bring to life,
That day when I can call on you proudly
    By the bright name of wife!

Away

You are away in Singapore,
    The city of your birth;
You are away in Singapore,
    A winsome spot of mirth!

You said you spent a merry childhood
    In that island of the south;
I blessed the place when these honeyed words
    First fell from your dear mouth!

You are among your kith and kin,
    Each day a fragrant flower;
You visit the shops and theatres,
    Enjoying the passing hour!

Glad at the thoughts that you are happy
    No loneliness I feel;
My love is to seek your summit welfare,
For which I will strive with zeal!

Initials

N stands for the beauteous nonpareil,
    Nonpareil,
    Nonpareil,
N stands for the beauteous nonpareil,
  With whom in love I fell!

K stands for the gay kaleidoscope,
    Kaleidoscope,
    Kaleidoscope,
K stands for the gay kaleidoscope,
  Which makes life shine with hope!

The other K stands for a kiss,
    For a kiss,
    For a kiss,
The other K stands for a kiss,
  Which is enchanting bliss!

Welcome Home

Enthralling is the air today,
    Enthralling is the sky of blue;
Luminous nature smiles serenely,
    The year begins anew!

An ineffable sweetness gleams in your eyes,
    An ineffable fragrance trills from your hair;
Radiant beauty glows in your face,
    Never was rose so fair!

To complete with you your journey home,
    Last evening, as I sat in the train,
I whirled away the sixty miles
    With fervid heart and brain!

Short though the parting was, to me
    The sun was shedding a decade's light;
I thought of you the whole day long,
    And dreamed of you at night!

Propitious is the air today,
    Propitious is the sky of blue;
Kindhearted nature smiles serenely,
    My life begins anew!

The Day We First Met

We two first met, my dearest,
    Exactly a year ago,
On the finest, happiest day
    The lunar year can show!

I felt a melodious meaning
    Enchant the evening air;
I thrilled with wonder and joy
    At beholding one so fair!

A year of radiant bliss
    Has been mine as never before;
My drifting boat had come
    To a sunny nook ashore!

Not only fair are you
    But good and wise withal;
How could I cease to love
    The star outstarring all?

'Twas an auspicious evening,
    Which brought us together, sweet;
And on its moonlit recurrence
    Its glory I joyously greet!

Wedding Day

This is the happiest morn of all
    That ever in my life has been;
This is the rosiest morn of all
    That ever my life has seen!

Oh sweetest, dearest—the star of my fate—
    Paragon of beauty and grace,
Of glorious wisdom and noble virtue,
    I live by your smiling face!

More than a year has fleetly elapsed
    Since I first beheld your beauteous brow;
I loved you then with the deepest love,
    And I adore you now!

That I would cherish you for aye
    On our engagement day I swore;
Now you are legally mine my feeling
    Glows tenderer than before!

I could not dream of passing the years
    Without you and your winsome smile;
Be lenient with my faults and make
    Our world a fairy isle!

Wedding Anniversary

Enchanting was the auspicious morn
    And blitheness thrilled the clear, cool air;
Close to my memory it nestles,
    That day so soft and fair!

When the wedding hour unfurled
    And I was yours and you were mine,
I looked into your eyes and felt
    My own with rapture shine!

A lovely bride without compare
    You were a year ago today;
You have become a wondrous wife
    As lovely, sweet, and gay!

The more I know of you the more
    The love that makes me cling to you;
Oh sweet! How constant is my heart
    The years will bring to view!

Today we celebrate our union
    Joyously in our pleasant home;
Merrily chirp the birds and merrily
    Glimmer the flowers in bloom!

Tanjong Bungah

From the cerulean vault above
Shoots the spherical energy its life-sustaining rays;
In burnished masses float cumuli,
Assuming forms begotten of fantasy,
Momentarily screening the solar disk,
Trailing off playful elves of wisps;
Bluest of blue skies,
Whitest of white clouds,
The tropical sun in resplendent glory—
Naught mars the enamouring dream of bliss!

Plays on the water light of gold,
The sea as far as eye can reach
An undulating green membrane,
Softest smiles exuding;
Blow light winds,
With delight dizzy,
Released from their nirvana of air—
Albeit moving within its vast expanse.

Brownish sands to left and right
Enjoy wakeful trance;
Beats life below them—
The tiny siput has its home;
By the water's edge grey rocks
The work of the ages reveal;
Stick cirripeds to their sides,
And crawl crabs around.

As lightly along the beach I stroll,
By wandering airs fanned,
Listening to the melody of the sea,
Mine is mellifluous blitheness
And serenity its honeyed essence distils;
Feel I the joy of the coconuts pendent
On the crown of the soaring trunks
Amid the swaying feathers of leaves!

Behind along the winding road cars flash,
In front around the sea boats cruise;
With holiday-makers bungalows teem,
Beneath umbrageous boughs their trade restaurants ply;
Free from woe looks the human scene;
Peace smiles the flower of the mind,
The flower of society no less;
Here all is tranquilly joyous—
Nature and man—
Elysium in this nook of space!

In a Rubber Plantation

In serried ranks they uprear
    Frames unromantic, straight—
Trees from whose furrows there creeps
    Latex of lacteal hue
In sheets to coagulate.

Here sunlight is a stranger,
    Gloomy and cold it feels;
One bane is blissfully absent—
    Bustle and tumult of streets
Its lips noise sulkily seals!

The Road

through the town
between the ridges of houses a trough
to the right gently swerving
to the left abruptly shooting
now straight as straight can be
the geometrical shortest distance between two points
thereon traffic clangorous incessant

land of fifty feet width
excavation here
filling there
roller rumbling giantlike
to camber moulded
thick spread of block metal
conversing through intervening quarry waste
rolling to concatenated case
course of asphalt macadam
rolling
another layer of black-coated smaller-size road metal
rolling
thus into existence the street

rigid like tradition
hard like typhoon
able to bear impact of fleet-wheeled automobiles
surface of sleek night
slight convexity
flanked by brothers of pavements
protected by sentries of concrete curbs
an umbrageous thoroughfare
its green verges glowing
with straight slender royal palms

spectacle
cars skimming up and down
pedestrians tripping along
this factitious line
on earth's surface
a work of scientific art
a peak of utility

without it
a town not a town
no circulatory flow of travel
simple its appearance
of magnetic glitter void
but in the scheme of things
of more consequence
than many a showy artifact

Reinforced Concrete

four measures of hardy granite
two of fine aggregate
one of Portland cement
water for correct consistency
whirling drum of concrete mixer
into it the separate ingredients
out the wet homogeneous mix

of steel bars an array
straight and bent
at right angles traversing
by thin wire restrained
framework within timber shuttering
pouring of concrete freshly mixed
grasping the steel

setting of the mass
its hardening with passage of days
liberation from prison of formwork
a solid grey fabric
of strength answering load envisaged

care over design
attention to diverse loadings
all manner of stresses
economy with efficiency the aim
care over execution
good quality of steel and concrete
fine scrupulous workmanship
sound safe structure the sequel

a wonder composite substance
two phenomena
in appearance as north from south
forming harmonious entity
with marvellous adhesion
its dual purpose
steel to combat tension
concrete to take compression
these conflicting forces
absorbed by one contrivance

different the mien of cities
without this unique material
extensive its use
piles and foundations
floors and walls
columns and beams
roofs arches and domes
a boon for bridges and buildings

advantages
lower cost than for its peers
resistance to fire
toughness against weathering
immunity against ruin by insects
a product of man
with utility crowned

utility versus beauty
both of need to world
no decrying of one
in name of other
nothing to hamper
utility evolving beauty

About the Author

Born around the time of the foundation of the Republic of China, in the former English colony of British Malaya, Tan Kheng Yeang was educated in an English school. His father was from China but had emigrated to Malaya and had become a successful businessman, involved in various activities, including as a rubber merchant. From his early days the author was interested in literature and philosophy and as his interest evolved to science, he decided to study civil engineering at the University of Hong Kong, as he felt he needed a practical career.

After the Japanese occupied Hong Kong, he went into free China where he found work in an office constructing roads and later an airfield in Guangxi Province. After the war ended in 1945, he returned to Malaya and became an engineer in the City Council of Georgetown, Penang. After his retirement, he worked as an engineering consultant. He is the author of twelve books that reflect the broad range of his interests and talents.